# MISERABLE @ W K

## STOP BLAMING THE JOB AND FIX WHAT'S REALLY BROKEN

11/17
M amman
blessings,
De. Wall

# STOP BLAMING THE JOB AND
# FIX WHAT'S REALLY BROKEN

Dr. Will Miller

**Niche Pressworks**

Visit Dr. Will on the web at www.drwill.com

Published by Niche Pressworks – www.nichepressworks.com

For permission to reprint portions of this content or bulk purchases, please email contact@drwill.com

ISBN Print: 978-1-946533-09-8
ISBN Digital: 978-1-946533-10-4

A person can do nothing better than to eat and
drink and find satisfaction in their own toil.
This too, I see, is from the hand of God.

Ecclesiastes 2:24


Love and work...work and love, that's all there is.

Sigmund Freud

# Acknowledgements

As will ever be the case, my most heartfelt gratitude is reserved for Dr. Sally Downham Miller, my wife, partner and advisor. Holding me to account with her expertise and wisdom, this book is a result of her insights and experience along with my own.

I also owe a debt of gratitude to my friend and colleague, Dr. Glenn Sparks, with whom I have collaborated on writing, research and a shared concern for the challenge of social isolation that is a worrisome reality of society today.

Dr. Tom Dukes, who has been a podcast partner and scholar collaborator helping me refine my teaching focus.

My thanks to my advisors extraordinaire, Nicole Gebhardt and Crystal Yeagy, who have guided this endeavor with energy and steady hands. And to my new buddy Maggie Petrovic who edited this mess.

And in memory and gratitude to my greatest generation parents: my father, Staff Sergeant William, for his heroic service during World War II and Helen, for modeling lifelong learning and passing along the snappy Irish wit.

# Table of Contents

# Introduction

I have never done anything especially heroic or extraordinary in my life. Nothing I've ever done has been featured on the evening news. Nonetheless, my pilgrimage has been interesting and diverse, to say the least. It's fitting that this whole story starts with the first- person singular. It is about me and what I have learned and desire to share.

Anyone who knows me, however, understands that I am not some condescending, arrogant sort, posing as a superior expert. Some may find me flakey, impulsive, rash, salty, profane and annoying. Yeah, perhaps all that...but not arrogant. I've often told people that my character was shaped principally by my mother and her posse of New York nuns.

I do trust the reliability of my moral compass. The insights that follow come from my own education, training and personal experiences as a white male, baby boomer with Attention Deficit Disorder and a Type A personality, living in this amazing place and time on earth.

When Eddie Murphy introduced me as the next act at The Comic Strip Comedy Club, he would say, "And now, I'm gonna bring up the whitest guy you ever saw!" As Popeye confessed, "I am what I am!"

It will offer insights coming from what's happened to me and what I learned as a psychotherapist, standup comedian, ordained Christian minister, professor and, to the point, a disgruntled worker myself. Throughout the years, I experienced fulfillment at some of my jobs for periods of time. And I've also been frustrated at some and knew I needed to change.

What I rarely experienced, however, is being miserable at a job but trapped without escape from it. I have enjoyed the luxury to make changes and flee to something else.

There are millions of people, however, who do not have this freedom. Some may lack enough education and training to enjoy much job flexibility and are often tethered to what feels like smothering responsibilities as parents and providers. I can feel compassion for such hardships but I have not endured them myself.

We all desire to live a great life. But, most are realistic that such may not be in the cards for us. Still, we want to have the balance that Freud described: being able to love and work and so cope with life's woes. As someone intensely curious about the state of modern society and culture, this is my offering about how to make this vision more attainable for both of us.

Over the years of my work as a psychotherapist and public speaker, I learned a lot about the work-life struggles of many Americans. Teachers, skill trade folks, lawyers, corporate executives, factory workers, sales pros, and police officers all tell tales of the disconnection between pride in their job mastery and the oppression felt at their job.

Whether it's the micromanaging supervisor, tone deaf top management, imperious, self-serving politicians, or the pressures from the community, so many are miserable at work.

A decade ago I began to work with area police departments as a chaplain and then eventually as a therapist and stress advisor for the officers. Coming in from the outside of this highly-insulated work culture, it was pretty obvious that there was a significant level of job frustration inside this profession as well. Policing is clearly a career to which someone is personally called. I've never met a police officer who, looking back, debated "Should I be an accountant or a cop?" No, in virtually every case I encountered, there was an early draw to this amazing line of work.

Much like the teachers, lawyers and electricians I know, cops take great pride in their professionalism and skill. It was a life goal for them that they often embraced when they were young. They don't express confusion or hesitancy about what they were responsible to do during their time on the clock. Their job miseries had surprisingly little to do with the work itself. The gripe is about the pressures impeding their freedom to do their job as they see fit. It's the oppressive nuisance of forces above and beyond their control that has soured many.

It's a sad case that many can rattle off exactly how much time they have left until they can retire. I will chronicle the career challenges of cops and teachers as illustrations of job stress in more detail in chapter two.

Who really knows how many Americans are miserable at work? What I propose in the coming narrative is an opportunity to stand back and look at one's life as an unfolding lifespan, climbing up out of the weeds that keep tripping us on our daily walk.

Therapists know that unlocking a complex life situation requires stepping back out from the emotion to see the escape paths more clearly. In doing so, I will attempt to tie together some apparently disparate social phenomena that are roiling America and our ability to love our labor.

I'll share what I have learned through my careers as a worker bee, a mental health professional, an entertainer with my fifteen minutes of fame, and a passionate learner throughout. The voice is mine, gleaned from this curious mix of life experiences.

My hope is that my assessment of the state of things will encourage you to renew your sagging optimism, recalibrate your perspective and restore your love for your life and labor. If you can embrace faith in the future it will revive your hope and reanimate your commitment and capacity to love. Let's carry on.

# CHAPTER 1

# Let's Meet Some Miserables

I've been involved in the work-misery business my whole career. Either appearing as a corporate speaker, a standup comedian or as a psychotherapist, each audience was listening to my insights about coping with daily life.

Whether it was a comedy routine about relationships, a motivating speech about life balance or a session trying to untangle the shambles of someone's personal life, the subtext was clearly some form of misery. But here I want to use the term misery with a small "m" to distinguish it from the capitalized model of … you know … BIG MISERIES.

Being miserable at work is more like managing a cold sore than dealing with an abscess tooth. It's about the stuff that drives you nuts and is your buzz kill.

Before we tackle the problems of America's troubled workers, let's flesh it out and start with a few individuals I've interviewed who have been miserable at work. And at the end of the book, I will share the steps they took to do something about it. I've changed their names but these are people I have known and whose stories I followed. Their tales of disillusionment caused me to think about what was happening to devoted, skilled workers who lost the joy and motivation for the jobs they once liked, if not loved.

Everywhere there are burned out teachers, nurses, cops, plumbers, electricians, cable company installers, sales professionals, surgeons and corporate executives. I'm long passed attributing work misery to some select industries and careers. It's everywhere and in every place. And the shrink in me wants to know why and what's going on here.

So, let's meet some miserables.

## Jack the Miserable Plumber

Jack is an expert plumber. He's mastered all of the basics of his field including the routine tasks of maintenance and crisis situations. His skill is beyond this, however, and he really loves designing systems and creating better ways to make things work.

He went to work for a large corporation and came in as the low man on the totem pole. Naturally at first, he got the worst, yuckiest jobs, which he expected as the new employee. It's the age-old reality of seniority over aptitude and skill. Yet, he believed that if he would just put in his time and impress his boss, he would get promoted.

BUT ... time after time he was "passed over" for promotions, which went to workers with less skill and commitment. The difference was that they had better inside connections. Each time a new job listing came up, he would get excited that this may be the moment for him. Then he would get the bad news. Each rejection was killing him. Yet, he was the one his coworkers and even his boss called in for emergencies, even when it was to help them out personally at their home.

He always went on his own time, again thinking this would count for him. But he came to despise his situation, his boss and the system. He still loved plumbing but felt impotent and demeaned in his work life. After a few years, he hardened, cared less, and only spoke the company name with impolite adjectives. His misery was written all over his face when asked about his job. He gave up hope and reacted with angry cynicism each time he was prompted to apply for another position.

Jack comes to work every day for every shift. Whether it's an annoying leak or a flat-out flood in a building, he gets the call. The helpless people in the messy muddle are always relieved when they see him. For Jack, it's not about the pipes; those are fun.

But it's that other stuff! Jack is miserable at work.

## Amanda the Miserable Teacher

Amanda is a renowned science teacher admired across the state. At county and state Science competitions, her students win the most blue ribbons, even though they come from a small school system. She is always on the front edge of her field, using the acronym STEM before most knew what it meant. She writes grants that get funded almost every year. She loves her job and relishes the competition to stay at the head of her field.

BUT ... In recent years, she and every other teacher are facing new, mandated testing requirements. These new assessment regulations are written by state legislators with little understanding of the life of teachers and kids in the classrooms. These new rules take away valuable time she used to have to focus on the science stuff she and her kids loved.

For Amanda, and most other teachers, the existing system may not have been perfect but it wasn't broken. Yet politicians took it upon themselves to fix things for her. She is indignant and bitter at the interference by unbending lawmakers. For the first time in her long career, she is a demoralized worker.

Amanda shows up every school day and looks with delight at the faces of her young students. She still attends to every activity and experiment with enthusiasm and excitement that is always contagious for the kids.

But it's that other stuff! Amanda is miserable at work.

## Sean the Miserable Cop

Sean has been a police officer for 14 years. He joined the force after leaving the Marines where he served a tour in Iraq. Like most of his colleagues, he loves being a cop and takes seriously the challenges that come with the mission.

It was a pretty smooth transition from the military to the "command and control" structure of law enforcement. And he has relished the extensive, ongoing training that is built into the job. He finds the wide variety of duties and assignments presented each day especially gratifying. He related how each day's shift featured unique challenges, from the controlled, physical aggression of an arrest to the empathy needed to help vulnerable victims. Sean loves the honor of serving as a police officer. "There's nothing like this job and I love what I do."

BUT ... the stressful pressures of the job are not often related to the police work itself. As Sean noted, "What I love about my job are the actual duties connected to police work." It's the peripheral matters that surround officers and intrude upon their work that bug Sean.

The agency's leadership, the bureaucracy, community pressures and modest salary are the variables that are the real source of distress for most officers. Having no control over these larger, overlaying matters is a thorn in their sides. They do a job that demands "command and control." It seems to be an intractable dilemma.

Sean puts on the uniform for each shift and goes about the routines of the day's issues and cases. He zeroes in on the department's daily priorities and assignments. He dutifully attends to entering the mountain of reports and filings that are part of his job. He's cool with all this stuff.

Sean still loves working in law enforcement, but it's the other stuff that so often leaves him feeling miserable at work.

## Nicole the Miserable Nurse Practitioner

Nicole is a supervising nurse at the hospital and is still exhilarated by the profession. She has an unquenchable passion for the emerging developments in health science which she believes are nothing short of "an incredible revolution." It makes her job exciting and she is filled with hope for her patients.

Since achieving the higher status as nurse practitioner, she has gained added status and authority. And she is especially enjoying the fulfilling partnerships she now has with the physicians with whom she works.

BUT … the misery for Nicole is, as you might imagine, in her words, "the insanity of the health system!" It intrudes and interferes with her team's goals and objectives for patient care. She's does not have any irrational illusions about the need for limitations in the system. But she observed that treatment recommendations are frequently stymied by the cold reality of insurance economics and patient resources.

What's worse is that decisions that interfere with medical judgement are frequently made by non-medical people concerned almost exclusively with bottom line implications. Interactions with the corporate system are frustrating and seems heartless to her and her coworkers.

Nicole soldiers on, trying to focus on each issue at hand and each patient she is seeing. Every case intrigues her to research and consult on every conceivable medical development. She tries to keep focused on the patients and not the obstacles. It's challenging to say the least.

Nicole loves her job, but it's the other stuff that makes her miserable at work.

## Geoffrey the Miserable Company President

All of Geoffrey's dreams have come true. He inherited the company his father started and earns multiple, seven figures a year. He has all the luxury possessions one can imagine. He is driven to the office each day to oversee his corporate empire and feels self-assured that he understands the company mission, product and market.

He regularly visits the factory and the workers down the power chain. His employees realize that he's there to chat and encourage them and they appear to find him sincere and likable. He loves his company. The company is his life; his life is the company.

BUT … as the CEO, every relationship he has there is limited, one-dimensional and shallow. He is surrounded by the obedient and the obsequious who report to him and depend on his favor for their success and even their livelihood. There is no one at the office who has mutual status in his world. He essentially has no real, authentic friends at work, just employees and underlings.

Geoffrey has mastered the art of presenting a confident face in public and inside the company. He has learned to limit his expectations for interpersonal gratification with the relationships there.

Geoffrey loves the people he works with, but it's the other stuff that makes him miserable at work.

## Will the Miserable Comedian

Like many professional comedians, Will came to the career from a previous profession. Having completed graduate school, he became a supervisor in the state's department of education. After about three years, Will got a call from his brother in New York who was regularly going to the comedy clubs in the city. He suggested that Will should try stand-up, reminding him that he had always been the funniest of all the seven siblings.

Bored, restless and newly divorced, Will quit his job and moved to the city, where he began the long, slow process of learning how to do standup. As he toiled away learning the strange skill, he took a day job as a high school teacher. He was in class during the day and nights at the "showcase clubs" that featured newcomers.

After accumulating enough material to be hired professionally, Will secured sufficient bookings to quit his day job and plowed ahead toward comedy fame. With a knack for writing bits and a flair for the spotlight, he soon established himself as a regular performer on the professional circuit.

He was liked and accepted by the comedy community and spent the next 17 years as a professional performer. He loved the stage and the craft. But the hitch for Will, as it was for all in the comic community, had nothing to do with performing itself. Even the nuisance of periodic audience hecklers and drunks was all part of the accepted, albeit irritating reality. The stage was not the issue.

BUT ... the real headache for comics is the business of comedy! And many aren't that adept at the skills required. Comedians have an amazing, strong bond with each other. They share an unusual experience and have deep respect for each other's journey, on stage, that is. Many don't do the off-stage stuff all that well.

Like all his colleagues, Will was at the mercy of the power and judgement of those who hire, support and create the necessary exposure. Television executives, booking agents, and club owners stand between the performer and the coveted audience. He had no beef with the stage. He was a polished professional who was booked every night as a featured act and eventually a headliner.

BUT … compared to many of his peers, however, he didn't possess the requisite talent for negotiating the business side of the system. He admits it was his own ineffectiveness promoting himself. Yet, it was this critical part of the job, the business of the profession, that made him miserable at work. Will plowed ahead doggedly for many years focusing on each audience at every club he worked. That part was great.

But it was that other stuff! Will was miserable at work.

Perhaps you can identify with the dilemma of these representative miserables. We will check in on developments in their misery saga later at the end. But, for now, the question is just how pervasive is this job misery issue? Is everyone struggling with all that "other stuff?"

So, what's really going on here? Is job misery limited and anecdotal or is it more of a widespread epidemic? Is it within some selective jobs and careers or is it really that pervasive? Let's take a closer look together.

# CHAPTER 2

# Job Misery: Anecdote or Epidemic

I realized early in life that I don't do delayed gratification all that well. If the now-common diagnosis of Attention Deficit Disorder had been around back then, I would have been on medication.

The approach my mother took was to tell the nuns at my Catholic School, "He's got the heebie-jeebies. I suggest you sit him in front."

So, my medication became a nun going "mano-a-nuno" with my mouthy self. And she could wield a yardstick like Zorro! This intervention was just as potent as Ritalin.

As an aside, I never liked the term 'deficit' which focuses on the disabling features of ADD. It doesn't reflect a can-do approach. I always preferred to use the word 'distraction' instead, because that's what it feels like. Holding still and focusing is a challenge.

Nevertheless, school was a 12-year sentence in white-collar prison for me. I managed to carry on and get by with lousy grades. But, I was constantly distracted and not focusing my attention.

A personal example was a dramatic incident when I was a kid in Catholic School. As early as the fourth grade, I was a veteran altar boy at St. Pius School. Occasionally, we were assigned to serve a funeral in the sanctuary next door, which meant a three-hour reprieve from the classroom. It was a cool perk that was sweetened by a gratuity from the funeral director. Sweet indeed! Living large at nine!

On one infamous occasion, however, in front of a packed house for the funeral of an elderly parish icon, I was not paying attention and my billowy surplus was lit up by my acolyte candle. The tall flames glowed on my cherubic face. I spun around and the pastor, Father Boyd, leapt up shrieking, "Glory be! The boy's on fire!" He and Father McKeever rolled me out on the floor, stood me back up with my black charred vestments and, nose to nose, whispered threateningly, "Now just stand there and be quiet." I refocused immediately. And because of the trauma, my attention probably lasted for another half hour. Distraction!

College was not a lot different. Graduation requires a GPA of at least 1.6 and to claim completion of one's major demanded a 2.0. My overall GPA from Providence College was 1.9 and my major, English, was a skin-of-the-teeth 2.03. Whew!

If school is seen as a job, then clearly, I was miserable at work. And, my attention issues have stayed with me my whole adult life.

While some may lament the road not taken in their life, it's obvious that I have always taken those other roads. It was either boredom with present circumstances or curiosity about a new adventure. I spend some time regretting my twitchy choices, but not much. What's pertinent here is that I have dabbled in a variety of work environments and have come away with some insights to share.

But more about me later. Now…

## Let's Talk About You

To deliberate about the life and complications of the modern American worker is a presumptuous endeavor. But, let's step back to take in the long view.

My experience, and the research is supportive, is that discontent with our jobs is real. The worried laborer with limited education and few flexible skills has analogous angst with the college-educated professional in education, nursing or management. So too with civil servants, first responders and mid-level government administrators. And, we should not leave out our captains of industry, watching with uneasiness the fluctuating trends of global economic vicissitudes that can quickly overturn their lifestyle.

Everybody is shaky. If some profess to be fine, let's ask them about how their children and family members are faring when they get together and talk about their lives at the holidays.

Assuming this resonates for you or your family, the issue here is why the work-life situation has come to a point of misery for you and so many others around you.

Without rehashing the research on the psychological state of American workers, data abounds about our general job disgruntlement. And it cuts across all demographics.

Some of the testimony shared here is anecdotal, but it isn't made up out of whole cloth. It comes from years as a psychotherapist and counselor, listening to people struggling with their lives and conflicts. After all, no one comes to a shrink to tell him how grand their life is, especially since we charge. If you identify with the premise that at some level you are, if not miserable, but just unhappy at your job, this book is for you.

The repeating lament about career and job is a common topic of discussion in any counseling practice. Is all this conflict confined to certain, predictably challenging careers? For quite a while, I was pretty narrowly focused on my clients who were typically college-educated individuals working in professional careers. It was teachers, lawyers, nurses, physicians and business executives who were coming to me. These were dedicated types who gave a great deal of their life energy to their calling.

Their initial problems were frequently about their relationships, most often their marriage and family. But when scratching the surface, in many cases, it was also real distress at their job.

Sometimes, work frustrations are repressed and then displaced somewhere else; most often directed at personal and family relationships. You know, barking at the people who love you, put up with you and usually forgive you.

Misplaced emotion inevitably exacerbates problems in family life, with incivility towards strangers, perhaps even some road rage. It becomes an issue of too much time at work and then neglecting family responsibilities. Or perhaps, it's too much focus on non-work interests, creating pressures at the job and thwarting potential for advancement and success. In all, it's life balance out of whack.

What is it? Are there so many individuals who are simply just disappointed and disillusioned with their choice of profession? Did they choose the wrong career path? Did they mishear their calling? Perhaps. But it doesn't end with this educated, professional demographic.

Surveys show that the majority of Americans are dissatisfied at work.[1] And the statistic cuts across the whole working population like doctors and factory workers, white-collar and blue-collar. Among the latter, most worker angst is about job

---

[1] Susan Adams, Forbes, 2014 http://www.forbes.com/sites/susanadams/2014/06/20/most-americans-are-unhappy-at-work/#326fe0995862

security. Worries include potential layoffs, company downsizing and relocation.

In what follows, we'll look at some of the larger trends that are evolving – or perhaps devolving – in America over the last half-century. It's not relegated to any one, single segment of society.

## More About Me

On my sixteenth birthday, my mother drove me over to King Kullen supermarket in Plainview, Long Island. She marched me over to the high counter and, without so much as a 'How do you do,' said to the manager, "Bobby, he's sixteen. When can he start?"

And so, the following Friday I punched in as an employee at the bottom of the food-service industry. My duties included unloading the truck, packing shelves, mopping the aisles and bagging for the cashiers. Being lowest on the totem pole, I was also the one called over the loudspeaker, "Billy, cleanup on aisle four."

Between tasks, I was told to get the mop and just, "Take off the bad spots" on the floor of the aisles. Soon, that was my moniker, 'Billy Bad Spots.' It didn't take long for me to advance to a checkout guy which was high prestige because it meant contact with actual customers and my own bagger!

I worked twenty hours a week, eight hours every Saturday and 12 more scattered across weekday nights after school. I made $1.15 an hour, which meant after taxes I was flush with a cool twenty bucks – every single week!

I was jubilant with the spike in my income, from the lousy eight dollars I took home from delivering 50 newspapers, seven day a week!

I was at King Kullen supermarket for five years, right through to the end of high school, and even a few summers home from college. It was the first of several jobs starting out. I branched out to being a delivery driver for Hill Florist, bringing flowers to funeral homes and housewives. This was a blast as I tooled around town in a cool Beetle Microbus, drinking coffee and smoking a cigarette all while operating the stick shift and steering with my knees.

I loved these jobs. Of course, I never had any illusions that they were careers. They were just jobs. I liked them and was good at them principally, because I had no burning instinct for rebellion. I was obedient and did what was told, just like at school and home. Well, actually, it was more so than at school and home where there was a modicum of behavioral wiggle room.

My life was balanced and in the organization of priorities, these jobs were obviously not my life's main focus no matter how many hours I clocked in at the place.

My mind was on other pursuits including the stress of school and my always disappointing social life. Popular culture was booming and I was fascinated by everything going on around me. At the time, the Beatles were singing "Help!" and Barry McGuire gave us the gloomy "Eve of Destruction." No, my job was just about money, albeit paltry. So, in my bones, I am from blue collar, working class roots.

## Back to You

Over the subsequent decades of my life and work, I have studied and paid attention to the correlation between individuals and how we cope with challenges common in modern life.

Acknowledging the context of the larger social realities is a critical variable to understanding people's problems. And the present social reality in America is complex, to say the least.

Despite the yearning for that elusive, better time we dream about for ourselves, it just doesn't feel like a promising new morning. It feels more like a mid-afternoon slump. Many feel unfulfilled with a flagging hope about our collective future, as well as our own personal prospects.

As noted, worker dissatisfaction is trending upward. Pessimism and angst seem pervasive these days. Wasn't the angry presidential election fueled by the helpless frustration that millions of Americans are feeling?

Political headlines may give a voice but do not clearly address the cause of our melancholy. This was really the coming eruption, or in shrink terms, of an emotional decompensation to a primal howl.

The manifest gloom has led so many companies to hire someone like me to come talk to their people about life balance, stress and quality of life. Even if the stated goal of the gathering is to increase sales, the underlying concern is morale, motivation and discontent.

While not every worker would describe themselves as miserable, surveys show that most are feeling less than fulfilled.[2] Most workers are, at best, bored at work.

Few, if any, career groups are immune. What is remarkable to me is the number of frustrated workers who tell me that they still love the actual work they are called to do.

One professor who quit his tenured, faculty position reflected on the common experiences in higher education with immovable, administrative bureaucracy and shrinking needed resources. His dissatisfaction had little to do with his scholarly passion for his field of study.[3]

Berkeley psychologist, Christina Maslach has studied worker burnout and documents its causes.[4] She reiterates that the lament is indeed not usually tied to the actual job task details. The factors that make work life stressful and overwhelming

---

[2]   Udemy Workplace Boredom Survey of 1,000 U.S. workers (2016)

[3]   Jonathan Malesic, *The 40-Year-Old Burnout: Why I gave up tenure for a yet-to-be-determined career* http://www.chronicle.com/article/The-40-Year-Old-Burnout/237979/

[4]   Maslach, C., & Leiter, M. P. (1997). The truth about burnout. San Francisco, CA:Jossey-Bass.

mostly include the lack of control over critical variables in your job, especially being marginalized from decision making.

And piling on, of course, is inept management of the workplace and social environment. It's the supervision that micromanages or ignores, and even enables worker conflicts. Sometimes the company or organization is simply a mismatch with one's values.

Worker misery can include the pace of a job. For some, there are unreasonable expectations of performance and an insensitivity to the need to balance work and personal life. When all this is combined with unrealistic expectations of commitment that consume someone's life and energy, it becomes a formula for morale problems at least, and high rates of attrition.[5]

My exposure to these various factors is seen in my therapy sessions. It is always a set of immobilizing symptoms that brings someone for counseling help. Let's be candid. Very few want to come to a shrink at the early onset of emerging symptoms. It's a move resisted until it cannot be ignored.

The suffering that immobilizes clients is classically connected to the current epidemic of anxiety and depression. They complain of agitation and irritability, headaches, insomnia and, not infrequently, alcohol and drugs – licit or illicit. Even when the complaints center on complex personal relationships

---

[5] Mayo Clinic Staff. (Sept, 2015). Job burnout: How to spot it and take action. Discover if you're at risk of job burnout — and what you can do when your job begins to affect your health and happiness. (http://www.mayoclinic.org/healthy-lifestyle/adult-health/in-depth/burnout/art-20046642

outside of work, scratching the surface reveals that job and career frustrations are in many ways the headline.

But, since there are few illusions of changing the workplace dynamics, the emotional displacement lands at home. What's going on here? Is this all just disillusionment and unrealistic expectations?

## Moi

Not everyone in low-skill, low-pay jobs is unhappy or even bored. Repetitive task jobs are appealing to some. Such jobs have their gratifications as long as the system remains stable and intact.

In the army, I was never disappointed to spend a day on KP – 'Kitchen Police' for the army cooks. This did not mean working as a sous chef for the head cook. It was the grunt work for the meal. I could peel hundreds of potatoes with ease while talking and laughing with my fellow soldiers. And the job was stable. I knew the army wasn't going to fold up the tent and move me to Mexico. I could have stayed in and found meaning in my low rank, with low pay and low responsibility.

But I never imagined that life for me. So much depends on the situation, influences and expectations instilled throughout childhood. My grocery store job was fine because it didn't in any way reflect or define my future ambitions. I never expected to be 'Billy Bad Spots' at forty. However, it was plausible that because I was smart – not yet highly educated, just smart – a career climbing the ladder in the grocery business could have been a good, viable fit for my life. Why not?

It did not occur to me until I was in college, that such a professional career path would be viewed as lofty. With a few exceptions, my classmates at Providence College in Rhode Island were from working-class families, and like me, were the first generation to go to college.

I was not aware of much condescension by "us" college-educated elite wannabes. In this generation of first-time college attendees, it was implied that we were fortunate. We were not just learning a new set of labor skills – I was an English major for heaven's sake.

It was the promise of lifting us up a notch in the social order, taking the baby steps from working class to middle class as a stopover, and moving on to the coveted social nobility of high achievers. And so, the fire of aspirations for greatness was ignited.

## Soldier On!

For the most part, we all just get up and walk on in our lives. There are so many people who are simply muddling along, distracted by whatever is going on in their life. And I'm not just talking about those who seek help where it's expected to hear their lamentations.

I've been a professional, traveling talker and listener for over 30 years. I've chatted up many thousands of people. Of course, even as they soldier on with life's complications, most are generally coping and perky. But there are so many who are miserable. They feel it in their personal life or their work life, often times both. I'm not necessarily talking about immobilizing, crippling misery. I'm not even talking about depression necessarily, although that indeed is a mental health epidemic.[6]

## My Bona Fides of Misery in Comedy

Whatever you are doing for your work, you understand the dynamics of the long trajectory for success or failure. A new teacher knows that there is a pathway to higher status if they choose. In order to climb the ladder of influence and money, the following steps need to be taken. You go get a master's degree in your spare time, take the state exams to become a school principal, then superintendent and then – who knows? The Secretary of Education? Even though most don't aspire to that experience, they all know the route to get there.

The same is true in any job. What does the nurse need to do? What about the lawyer, surgeon and sales professional? The kid stocking shelves in the grocery store and the woman on the factory floor all know the pathway to the top if they want it. Even the cops know the way to chiefdom. There are few surprises on how the system is structured. The opportunities are usually there for the motivated and the dedicated.

When thinking about the job of a standup comedian, you might not associate it with this misery at work theme. And of course, you would be wrong.

---

[6] World Health Organization: Depression Depression Fact Sheet. Feb. 2017. http://www.who.int/mediacentre/factsheets/fs369/en/

I devoted two decades of my adult life to standup comedy and had, I'll bet, the same mixture of joy and buzzkill as you have in your line of work. And I will tell you the cause of my misery has more similarities than differences to you.

For beginning comics, you have to work up the nerve to try it and to understand what being a standup comic generally entails. In a nutshell, it's signing up for several years of early humiliation and failure, followed slowly by a crawl into competency and then onto confident mastery.

There is a fundamental distinction that should not be lost on anyone thinking about a career path in the nightclub environment. From the outset, you recognize the obvious difference between making your friends and family laugh and learning to make strangers laugh. There is virtually no similarity; they're an ocean apart.

Even being the funniest guy at the office doesn't capture the predicament of winning a group of diverse club patrons, skeptical of your ability and well-oiled with alcohol. Jerry Seinfeld said it best when observing that the problem with standup is that it is actually theater that got misplaced in bars.

Yessiree.

But this again is what you must know before you get up there. You accept you'll be anxious, even terrified despite a brave face. You are all alone.

I've often told people what's amazing is not that you got up there the first time. Determination, courage and brashness can do that. What's amazing is getting up the second time.

In my first experience, I did a routine on the Kennedy assassination. Really. It was mocking the Warren Commission findings with some wiseacre cracks. I lasted roughly five minutes, and got about three chuckles. That was enough for me, I was off to the races. Doing my act onstage was exhilarating and I loved it! And, I even believed I knew what was in store for me, going forward. Or so I thought.

My first out-of-town job was at the Pittsburgh Comedy Club. It was a Thursday through Sunday gig; five shows and I was the emcee. It was my third year of full-time performing and the first time I left the New York area clubs. I was so excited as I got on the plane. The opening act was T.P Mulrooney from Chicago, and the headliner was Jay Leno.

I was ecstatic to work with Jay. He was already a legend in the comedy world, although his mainstream fame was just beginning to take off. I had the opportunity to learn at the feet of the master! And Jay was always a great, generous friend to comics, encouraging and inspiring. His own story was legendary among us. A brilliant stage comic with amazing material, he had his own series of rejections. One time he was told that he wasn't right for a television sitcom because his face would – get this – "scare children!" Every performer has a story of misery.

We were in the Green Room before the first show, and T.P. was telling Jay he was frustrated with his career. Jay asked, "How long you been working?" T.P. said he'd been at it about five years. "Do you work every night?" Leno asked. "Yes, every night."

Leno's response had me enthralled. "Okay, that means you are just learning who you are onstage." We both leaned in with, "What do you mean?"

Jay went on, "It takes five to seven years of nightly performances to figure out your identity on stage as a comic. That begins the process of selling that character."

I was pinned! It made perfect sense. Jay Leno's signature persona was developed over a decade of performing, and it was just then, in the early eighties, that he started being noticed and followed.

Well there I was, three years into it and being reminded that I was at the beginning of the beginning. And what comforted me was my reaction of acceptance that mastering the job was a long process. As Richie Tienken, legendary owner of the Comic Strip used to remind us, "Remember, it's a marathon not a sprint."

What I didn't master was the business of show business. How to negotiate the politics and relationships of the massive bureaucracy of the industry. Insanely competitive and heartless, it takes denial or the ego of a narcissist, to carry on with the early stages of the career.

So how is it done, how did we cope emotionally in this insanity? Sound like a familiar question for you in your job? It's not the job. It's all the other stuff. We did it by being together with each other. I stayed with it and loved it because I came to love my comrades in comedy.

The bond created among us was, and still is, like super glue. There were some frictions with a few of the personalities but, among the hundred or so who were working in those early days of the New York comedy boom, not many to speak of, actually.

No matter what style of performance you had – observational like Seinfeld and Paul Reiser, high-energy like Robin Williams, deadpan like Steven Wright or a music act, we hung together, laughed at each other and shared the same stage each night. And, we even commiserated about the trials of trying to get noticed, get booked and pay the rent.

There was only one unforgivable sin and that was stealing material. Other than that, it was a family and it was a blast. But there was misery, plenty of it, that had nothing whatsoever to do with the joy of performing our acts. The misery ain't about the job!

# CHAPTER 3

# The Skinny on Stress

Regardless of what job or career you are in right now, whatever misery you are feeling is shared across a wide swath of the working population. I can make the case that there is more similarity to what causes work distress than there are differences.

The computer programmer, realtor, airline pilot, physician and CPA share a striking commonality in their frustrations. In a word, it's about the stress they experience with parts of the job that are usually peripheral to the tasks being performed.

It is, as I often hear, "the other stuff" that's driving them nuts. And, as I pointed out, this even includes comedians. We are all stressed. But what exactly does this mean? It's about that bright red river flowing through your body. We're talking cortisol people.

Cortisol, those destructive little hormones bathing in our blood, are associated with all manner of worrisome consequences.

Recently, I took part in a new health initiative, on diabetes, as a board member of my area YMCA and our local hospitals. I was stunned when they said that almost 30 million Americans have Type 2 diabetes, but less than 10 million know it! And if you add those in the category of "pre-diabetes," the number spikes to an astonishing 90 million![7] If stress is a factor in raising our cortisol count and increases our risk for blood-connected physical symptoms, then it's past time to address the stress.

I recall reading a book about the Type A personality by a physician expert from Duke University. As unbelievable as it seems to me now, I never identified or thought of myself as Type A. My awareness of it was so vague that I actually thought of it as a positive. You know, smart, alert and assertive. I never connected being tense, impatient and short-tempered to the risks of this personality type.

In fact, the author labeled this the "Coronary Personality!"[8] Of course, I was wired as tight as a tourniquet, but believe it or not, I actually thought these traits were primarily assets for me. I attributed my energy, creativity and humor to these features of my personality. I didn't think of myself as being at risk for stress. And what did that mean anyway – to be "stressed"?

Telling someone that you are "stressed out" is pretty useless. The word, that is, not the phenomena. The term is inherently meaningless but we use it sincerely to communicate our worries

[7]  http://www.diabetes.org/diabetes-basics/statistics/?loc=db-slabnav
[8]  https://www.ncbi.nlm.nih.gov/pubmed/3681651

and anxieties. It describes a feeling of some helplessness to settle ourselves down. We use "stressed" to talk about the discomfort we're feeling and attribute it to some event, relationship, job or our life situation in general.

Like many in the counseling profession, awareness of the significant physiological impact of stress, came later in my career. While trained to focus on the psyche, the flood of brain research in the past thirty years has consumed every facet of the counseling profession. Despite the imprecise term we so casually use, the implications for both our physical and mental health are profound.

Today health professionals focus on the symptoms that result from our stressors. Something is obviously bugging you, but the pertinent issue is, "How are you reacting to it?" Are you stoic, perhaps repressing the discomfort? Are you having physical symptoms that appear to be unrelated to your emotional complaint?

The array of manifestations is myriad, including insomnia, anxiety, depression and often gastrointestinal symptoms. So, these body reactions are piled on top of the emotional miseries we experience. Sadness, despair and helplessness are the mind-consuming thoughts that trap us and do their work on our bodies.

It's with the symptoms that the rubber meets the road when addressing stress. You may not be anywhere near this level of crisis, but knowing the trajectory of unrelieved stress is really important.

To say that your mind and body work in close concert is an understatement. That stress you have been enduring, likely heroically, is having an impact on your body. The spirit may be willing to endure, but the flesh is maddeningly weak.

It brings to mind that familiar term "psychosomatic." This is often used derisively by someone, like your father, while barking dismissively at one of your sob stories. He may not use the technical term, but saying to you, "Come on, it's all in your head," is the same thing.

Well, not so fast, Commander! That word psychosomatic is describing a mental matter (psyche) that is affecting your body (soma). Ulcers are psychosomatic, as are high blood pressure and most anxiety symptoms. Some research even suggests that some cancers are connected to stress.

It's a situation where your mind is driving spikes into your body. The fact is, a staggering percentage of physical symptoms that are treated by a physician have a psychological root cause![9] Our body is profoundly shaped, altered and worked on by our mental state. So yes, we have to talk about stress, despite the word being way overused.

Over the years, I have been hired to deliver keynote speeches to groups about coping with stress. To tell your conference attendees that there will be a morning presentation on stress,

---

[9]   https://www.psychologytoday.com/blog/happiness-in-world/201003/psychosomatic-symptoms

many just roll their eyes and are grateful to have their smartphone discreetly on their lap during the talk.

In defense of us traveling sermonizers, many in the audience have merely a generic grasp of the organic impact of stress. Although not a scientist or medical professional, my therapy practice addresses the matter – ever and always.

Whatever your particular psychosomatic manifestations, life routinely confronts us with situations that can defeat us. We feel these setbacks in forms that essentially slow us down, even stop us. Left unattended, the impact on both body and mind surely contribute to our epidemiology of serious mood disorders, like anxiety and depression.

Whether these are firmly entrenched in one's physical makeup or brought on in reaction to life setbacks, the damage to health is unmistakable. This issue is so serious that the World Health Organization named depression as the number one health crisis in the world![10]

After my annual physical, the doctor's written report shows detailed data about my condition, that is essentially indecipherable. It is a page of letters, numbers and fractions that only the medical professional could decipher. And virtually all this information was revealed and categorized after analysis of the blood I gave at the lab.

---

[10]    World Health Organization Report on Depression

I had no idea what it said, but was satisfied with the doctor's summary about my overall health and any possible alarms it raised. It was simply trust in the professional's interpretation.

One time, my doctor alarmed me by asking how much alcohol I drank. When I asked why, he ominously said, "I don't like your liver number." Whoa! A bad liver? I almost asked out loud, "How much time do I have left?" Well, it turns out to have been a misunderstanding. He based his worries on an earlier interview report, which said that I had about five to seven drinks a week, but mistakenly wrote that I was doing that every day! I tried to correct him, but the liver number said it all. I was unnerved and became anxious about my habits and my liver!

Some months later, at a visit to my new doctor, he frowned when I told him this and said my liver number was normal. Turns out that the other doctor was a teetotaler who was evidently on a little mission. Whew! But it was a lesson about my need to learn about all those numbers and fractions describing my blood's health.

Blood tells the story about health in time and place. If the eyes are the window into the soul, blood is the pipeline into the guts. Modern diagnostics use our blood to evaluate the status of our organism, both generally and in particular. Those dreaded follow-up calls from the doctor's office that they "found something", cause us stomach-churning fear and torment while we wait for the details.

## My Lesson Learned

I'm an unlikely survivor of the infamous "widow maker" – sudden cardiac arrest, or as the surgeon called it, "sudden cardiac death."

On a beautiful August day in 2009, I was sitting in my office, two long hallways from the front door and main entrance. I had no evident symptoms and no family history, so the idea of my heart preparing to suddenly shut down was not on my radar. I felt none of the known warning symptoms at all.

I was at my desk reading and, for some reason, to this day I have no idea why, I strolled down to the front office and said to the office manager, "I don't feel…" At that moment, I went completely blank. I fell head long and smashed my head on a metal doorjamb and the concussion knocked me out.

My heart was one hundred percent blocked! I was turning purple when they called 911. Officer John Watson of the West Lafayette Police Department, happened to be on the corner and was first there. He gave me chest compressions to restart my heart, but I wasn't responding.

Miraculously, the firehouse was only two doors away from the building and within that brief survival window the first responders, my life-saving heroes began defibrillation. I coded three more times in the ambulance before I got to the hospital. Dr. George Brodel put a stent in my heart's descending aorta and, incredibly, I was saved.

Now here I am years later, alive and functioning and writing. Sometime afterward, I told Jason, the Police Chief, that I never had a Near Death Experience or saw the famous 'light' when I was out. I mean here I was, dying inside a church building and I'm a minister. But nothing! Bupkis!

The chief's theory was that Officer Watson was blocking it. It's always made me wonder what post-traumatic stress means when you have no memory of the trauma. I have zero recall. But I digress.

Since that episode, I've had to educate myself more fully about coping with the correlation between stress and physical well-being, especially since groups were paying me to provide insight about the topic. Now let's turn to something relevant and curious – let's discuss baboons. The most helpful insights into the matter of stress for me came from two remarkable experts: Professor Robert Sapolsky and Psychologist Kevin Gilmartin.

## Sapolsky & The Baboons

Talk about an individual with ornate and complex titles, Stanford professor Robert Sapolsky takes the cake. He is both a "primatologist" who studies apes, gorillas and monkeys, as well as a "neuroendocrinologist" who studies the interaction between the central nervous system and the endocrine system. He is a true legend for his pioneering work on stress. In particular, he helped clarify and establish the distinction between acute and chronic stress and their impact on our health. His book, with the title I love, *Why Zebras Don't Get Ulcers*,[11] details the thesis that their bodies are designed with the capacity to recover from an acute stressor, with minimal lingering damage.

The zebras calmly graze and hunt food until suddenly, there is a lethal predator attacking the herd. Running for their lives, the episode ends with the capture of one, allowing the rest to return to calm. Bodily systems return to their quieted state and grazing goes on for them. It's the common tale of evolutionary adaptation to living with regular, but intermittent threats to survival. It's an existence of life or death with not much in between the two.

Following his suspicions, Sapolsky set out to demonstrate that the human body can also stand up to acute fight or flight episodes without permanent, organic damage, even when the psychological impact is significant and lasting. His assertion was that we are poorly designed to withstand the corrosive effects of chronic stress.

He set out to demonstrate this in his renowned studies in Africa with baboons. He chose them because, first of all, they do bear a disturbing resemblance to us all. In addition, baboons, like us, live in a highly complex social environment. Their life is centered around their interactions with the others in their community (or "congress" as it is laughingly known in academic circles).

---

[11]  Sapolsky, Robert. *Why Zebras Don't Get Ulcers* (1994, Holt Paperbacks/Owl 3rd Rep. Ed. 2004) ISBN 0-8050-7369-8

A key feature of the baboon group is its strong alpha-male social structure. The alpha at the top rules over layers of the dominated others down to the females. All others find their place in the hierarchical system. The alphas rule and the dominated cope. Sapolsky theorized that the alpha males would experience the least amount of chronic stress as evidenced in the health of their blood.

By comparison, he believed that other, non-alphas in the community would display clear and varied levels of stress hormones. This would be the result of the persistent tension attendant to their vigilance to survive. This is not really a surprise to us intuitively; it's good to be the alpha!

The research did indeed confirm through blood samples that the alphas had measurably lower cortisol compared to their dominated primate family. And, by the way, the blood was collected by his Stanford graduate students who anesthetized the beasts using blow-gun darts to safely take the samples!

The theory was supported that the less chronically stressed they were, the lower their cortisol count, the healthier their blood. And the correlations also proved true. The farther down the dominance tier they were, the poorer the health outcomes, as revealed again in their blood samples. His research persuasively supported his idea.

This research approach was utilized in a study of humans in the Whitehall Study in London.[12] The civil service bureaucracy in

---

[12]    http://unhealthywork.org/classic-studies/the-whitehall-study/

England is also structured as an analogously hierarchical system. Those in authority are at the top, overseeing layers of worker levels, down to those with the least responsibility and power.

Sapolsky continued to collect relevant data over 30 years studying the same community of primates. In a unique and chilling account, one summer during their annual research visit, there was a crisis in the community. The baboons had come upon a deserted human camp where there was abandoned and decayed food. Predictably, the alpha males were the first to get and consume the rotted food and it killed several of them.

The remaining group of non-alphas survived and an amazing transformation occurred in the culture of the colony. With few or no alpha males, the remaining community thrived with far less internal conflict.

Beyond the curiosity of this research, the implications for human beings are significant. We are, it's clear, poorly designed to survive under the pressure of chronic stress. I came to appreciate this research especially when I started working with the police.

## Gilmartin & Police Vigilance

About a decade ago, the area Police Departments asked me to serve as a volunteer chaplain. Many, if not most, police agencies utilize chaplains to support their mission. The responsibilities of a chaplain can include counseling for the officers. A notable duty is accompanying officers when doing a death notification. This, as you can imagine, is a most difficult and onerous detail for them. As one officer friend noted darkly, "Man, I'd rather take a beating than do a death notification!" There's just no upside to the experience. So it's helpful for the officer to be accompanied by a chaplain.

When you go with an officer in the middle of the night, knock on someone's door and inform them of the death of a loved one, it's brutal. When they answer the door and see a police officer, they know it's bad news. But, when they see another person with "Chaplain" in big letters across their jacket, they know it is dreadful news, but of a different kind.

The predictable emotional outburst that inevitably erupts can be unnerving, to say the least. When some of this reaction can be directed toward the chaplain, it eases the stress on the officer. After all, chaplains are trained for this kind of encounter.

All these encounters are traumatic, obviously for the victims but for the officers as well. Sometimes the reactions are so emotional they become violent, acting out. More typically they involve people collapsing and dissolving into tears.

Some are really unpredictable as was the case when I accompanied an officer to a local office to inform a woman that her father had died. She was stone faced for a long moment and then said bluntly, "good." We were the ones reacting and I sheepishly offered, "It was a complicated relationship I take it?" Her reply was, "Yeah, he was a rat". Wow! Every day officers encounter the emotional, the unpredictable and the shocking. My respect for the job they do could not be higher.

Beginning with the chaplain function, my involvement eventually deepened with the departments, using my background and training as a therapist and stress consultant. This has been a far better fit for me, of course, and it has given me access into the unique culture of law enforcement.

It became obvious that my public speaking content was highly relevant to law enforcement professionals. Police officers are living the Sapolsky Thesis every day. So, while I was speaking nationally on stress to executives, I needed to do a crash course on its relevance to police. That's where I came across the work of Dr. Kevin Gilmartin.

Dr. Kevin Gilmartin is a legend in the world of police officer health and well-being. He was a police officer himself for many years in Arizona, who became a psychologist with special research interest in officer stress. His book, *Emotional Survival for Law Enforcement,*[13] is virtually a must-read for all police and their families. It is the primary reference resource I use when counseling in the local agencies. It's a blunt analysis of the risks involved in this most unusual career calling.

While there certainly may be exceptions, each officer knew what they were signing up with the motive to protect and serve. Some made the transition from military to police where the

---

[13]  Gilmartin, Kevin (2002). Emotional Survival for Law Enforcement.

discipline and ideals point to public service. After completing training, there is little hesitancy or confusion about the specific tasks involved. They feel ready and determined to perform – whether it's an arrest, investigation, or taking charge of a car accident scene with authority and proper compassion.

Gilmartin makes clear that it is not the "cop stuff" that creates the pervasive problems that officers experience. The data is tragic and telling. Police officers lead almost all other professions in divorce, addiction, suicide and early death. His thesis is compelling that the underlying issue is the failure to acknowledge and treat the chronic stress inherent in the job.

Taking a page from the Sapolsky research, police officers are routinely exposed to high-stress situations. They experience acute stress within themselves at many calls, and they are certainly engaged with citizens who themselves are in the middle of an acute crisis.

As Sapolsky observed, when an acute crisis ends, our bodies generally recover. In contrast, however, what is especially debilitating is the corrosive, chronic stress inherent in the police career.

Gilmartin coined the term "hyper-vigilance roller coaster." The hours during a tour demand a level of psychological vigilance, that never really comes to full rest during the job. Officers go from high alert to a ready alert between incidents. He then contends that upon finishing their work shift, officers return home and often crash in a completely depleted state. He uses the phrase "the magic chair" to describe a police officer vegetating in their recliner, watching television to decompress.

The consequences of this include pressure on their family relationships. It is here that their state of utter emotional and physical exhaustion can easily be misinterpreted as emotional distance and apathy. Combine this with the well-known stereotype that officers are notorious for not sharing details of their job with their spouse and family, but almost exclusively with other officers. It's a perfect storm of emotional detachment and relationship conflict

Upon reflection from these two scholars, I gained insight into the root of the stress dilemma for police officers. Although this is an extreme example, it applies to other job stress situations for many others. For those who are called upon to be alert and vigilant throughout their work day with too few interludes of rest, it takes a toll and robs us of the energy we need for our life away from the job.

The tasks of your job may not include having to become physically aggressive or taking charge of a chaotic scene, but it almost certainly includes attending with focused alertness to the demands put upon you throughout the day.

Whether you are feeling the pressure of closing a sale, fixing a glitch on a manufacturing line, responding to a defiant student in the classroom or a patient in your ward whose alarm is going off, you may deal with a hyper-vigilance roller coaster at your job as well.

White-collar or blue-collar, high-octane leader or simple worker bee, every job has demands and we know we are capable of their mastery. And just like the cops, it's often less about the job stuff but more significantly about the pressures and stress attendant to the relationships, management and leadership. Even if it's at a lower intensity level than a police officer, can you relate to the dynamic of the hyper-vigilance roller coaster and the magic chair waiting for you at home?

# CHAPTER 4

# Our Fragile, Mortal Infrastructure

If you're reading this book, perhaps it's because just seeing the title made you twitch. Or maybe someone close to you thought you should read it. In any case, it's a sad truth that millions are miserable at work to varying degrees of intensity.

Before we get to some solutions, allow me to share insights about factors that might be playing into your frustrations. They come from personal and professional experience from someone muddling along through life, just like you. It's comes from years of formal study and countless hours as a therapist, as well as spending time in therapy myself. I have some ideas to share about the dilemma of the American worker. Hopefully you will find this review instructive, because it's all about...well...you and me.

For starters, allow me to go to confession. I assume you are familiar with the idea. In the faith business, confessing is the act of stating my shortcomings out loud to another. In doing so I feel relief. But, in order for it to really have a curative effect, the transgressor must – and this is the critical part – do penance or pay back for the transgression.

It's an ancient and slick system that has good psychological footing. All the big religions have it in their own way. Catholics go to a priest, Jews acknowledge it during Yom Kippur, their Day of Atonement, Islam has its penance traditions. I don't know what the snake handler churches do.

As a kid in Catholic School, I was introduced to the practice of confession in about the second grade. Looking back, I understand the motivation, encouraging truthfulness and remorse. It's a fundamental lesson for life about having the courage of disclosure and shame for misdeeds (trespasses in the vernacular).

It's undeniable that societies depend on this system of taking responsibility for our actions and living with an active conscience. Lacking a conscience is the hallmark of a sociopath and, in general, that's really bad. It's organized religion's way of setting the standard for all human behavior that enables personal peace and social harmony

For me, these standards were already in place in my home. I was a lot more anxious about the penance my mother would dole out than that of the priest shadowed behind the screen in the dark booth. In fact, I often had trouble remembering my list of sins due to be reported at weekly confession.

It was no small irony that in order to be holy and revealing, I would confess to some sins I was not sure I actually committed. I would say I lied five times, but it was a guess. Then, I left absolved yet knew I had told a lie in the confession. Put that on the 'to do' list for next week's session. It wasn't easy being a Catholic kid.

## What Are We Anyway?

Before we talk about who we are as individuals, let's consider what we are as creatures. As an aside, I found it fascinating when, in a class lecture on The Book of Genesis at Union Theological Seminary, Professor Phyllis Trible noted that the word commonly translated as 'man' is better rendered as 'the creature.'[14] It's a bit deflating being reduced to that designation. Whatever we choose to call ourselves, it can be said confidently that human beings are a marvel of creative design that features a frail psyche inside an eggshell.

We spend an enormous amount of our time and energy, either trying to figure out life or finding ways to distract us from this baffling endeavor. Choosing to scrupulously avoid thinking deep thoughts about the meaning of the human existence is understandable because … well … it's just so not understandable. But I wholeheartedly recommend the activity for everyone.

---

[14]  https://theology4me.wordpress.com/2012/03/11/eve-and-adam-genesis-2-3-reread-phyllis-trible-copyright-1973-by-andover-newton-theological-school/

Socrates was an ancient Greek superstar who influenced centuries of western philosophical thought about ethics, community and social order. He was put on trial for "corrupting the youth of the city-state and impiety against the pantheon of Athens." The trial was like an ancient reality show and he was sentenced to death by drinking poison.[15]

During the proceedings, the court reporter saved for all time his famous words, "the unexamined life is not worth living." This timeless maxim is a word to all of us asserting that human contentment comes most fully through introspection. Now honestly, it might also be said that, in my experience, the overly reflected life can be tortuous. Nevertheless, I believe that being a completely unreflective blockhead is not conducive to emotional well-being.

It is worthwhile thinking about what it is you think about – yourself, your life, your very existence. I know it sounds heavy, but again, indulge me. You don't need to tell anyone else and there will be no crying, unless you would like to cry.

No, this is about what I've learned through a lot of navel-gazing. This bizarre phrase just means staring at your belly button and contemplating the meaning of your life. Yeah, I realize how wacko that sounds. Anyway, let me share with you what I have learned through several decades of navel gazing, combined with a lot of formal education and practice.

---

[15]    Trial of Socrates. (377 BCE). https://en.wikipedia.org/wiki/Socrates

## Now You

My guess is that the word "neurotic" is somewhere in your vocabulary. It's been used by you to describe others or by others talking about you. Describing someone as neurotic is not a compliment, but what exactly does it mean? In a word, it means sensitive, I suppose. The best definition I've heard is that it's the inability to keep your thoughts in the present moment. They tend to drift forward with anxious worry or ruminate back to past worrisome situations.

The ideal is to keep yourself in the present moment. Easy to say, but it can be done. When perpetually ruminating about past or future stressors, our whole organism and its fidgety systems feel the effects.

This intricate interaction between physical and psychological is a big historical change in the science. In times past, humanity was commonly viewed dualistically; the body and soul as distinct entities (to be politically correct we now say psyche instead of soul).

For most of history, the psyche and the soul were essentially synonymous. Think of Shakespeare's line about the body and death: when we "shuffle off this mortal coil." Well guess what? The coil is intertwined through you and not just wrapped around you. The familiar phrase body, mind, spirit is no longer relegated to us airy-fairy types. It is now embedded in science.

The practice of all helping professions, from medicine to psychology, now follows a course of engagement known as the "BioPsychoSocial approach" to assessment. As the tangled term indicates, diagnosis takes into consideration all parts of us: physical, mental and social.

When someone comes for treatment with a problem, it's standard to rule in or out any organic factors (bio), psychological considerations (psycho) and then relationship matters (social). It's a neat pathway to understanding what's going on and what can be done to fix it.

Keep this in mind when thinking about your own symptoms. Are your physical symptoms driven by your anxiety? Are your worries about jobs and family life behind troubles with your insomnia? Are they driving your cranky irritability? Well, hello, of course they are! Is your chronic fatigue, isolation, sad mood and screwy appetite correlated with your depression? Yes. Remember the 'psychosomatic' reference a chapter ago? Stating the obvious, how you are thinking drives your organism, physically.

It stands to reason that working on your thinking patterns, "cognition" in shrink speak, is a pathway out for some of what's ailing you. Human beings are meaning-making creatures – the interpretations we make are consequential for making changes. It argues for a life of some deeper reflection.

If the rest of your life is generally gratifying, even with the typical frustrations of family relationships, then misery at work is something you probably just put up with and try to tolerate. But just putting up with, and tolerating a daily grind that's part of your inescapable routine is like enduring a toothache. It's the part of your life that's a mood buzz-kill; something you'd rather put out of your mind as soon as you start the car or hop on the bus or train to head home.

If this describes your dilemma, that the issue is not really about your work functions specifically, then what's the problem here? Simply put, it's that segment of your work day that you just can't control and change. Suffering under the thumb of a narcissistic, micromanaging bonehead boss is not a changeable variable. Your only hope, usually a fantasy, is that this irritating jughead will irritate someone above them and get reassigned or, better yet, the boot.

When those magic moments do happen, the entire culture of the workplace changes instantly. But again, we're dealing in fantasy and it's not something you likely can make happen.

For the moment, let's pause chewing on your job misery dilemma. Admitting that you are "miserable at work" is a gloomy confession. But it is surely a common, even pervasive lament. And it's a discontent we guard against ever revealing to our boss. We do frequently share our aggravations and anger with family, friends and, of course, our bitter, dispirited co-workers. Exasperation with our jobs is a troubling psychological dilemma, especially when you don't foresee a change in the situation.

Like anything that causes us angst and discomfort, we usually can rattle off the reasons for our distress. Across all manner of careers and jobs, there is a common recitation of aggravating factors like the bureaucracy, the management, the customers, clients…on and on. Very rarely do I hear complaints about the actual tasks the job demands.

Aggravated sales professionals usually still relish the challenge of client persuasion. Cops are rarely confused about the core cop stuff. Surgeons still remain passionate and focused on cutting and sewing. Factory workers usually take pride in the efficiency of the machine they operate. Accountants still get a rise out of numbers and data, and teachers still care about the kids in their charge.

I recently visited a friend in the hospital and a nurse snapped at me for pressing her for medical information. I made her day a little more miserable even as she was expertly and happily checking tubes and monitors around the patient. I'm betting you could make the same claim about your own job. So, to the degree that this is generally true, it is often not about the work itself. Evidently, it's other stuff.

Let's back away from the particulars of your grievances. Is there a way to rethink this, to reframe what might really be going on beyond your own certainty about what's causing your headaches?

Confronting a life problem that appears to elude your control, brings out the normally resistant urge to get some insight, if not actual help. A standard approach in counseling psychology is obviously to begin exploring the specifics of someone's complaint. In response, the therapist tries to pull back from the aggravating details, what are called the 'presenting problems' and take in the bigger picture of a client's life.

It's all about context. The irritating problem that brings you to counseling needs to be seen in larger context. It's this approach that gives rise to the cliché about the therapist who always wants to start with, "Let's begin by talking about your mother."

When the opening words of the therapist appear to be off topic and intrusive, it can become a deterrent for people to even try counseling therapy. "Hey, Sigmund. I came here for you to help me solve my current problem, not a trip down memory lane!" Sharing my life openly with a stranger who, by the way, charges by the session is decidedly unappealing to many. It's the apprehension people have about the stereotype of the therapist. All I can say in our defense is that we can't help it.

## Let's Think Shrink

We instinctively seek relief from our runaway thoughts. How we seek that relief is varied and hugely consequential. You can find ways that are both adaptive and maladaptive. The relentless scourge of substance abuse is testimony to the millions who are taking this option. A psychiatrist in New York shared with me the philosophy and approach he takes with substance abuse. He said, "Here we use a simple definition of addiction; it's an impulse to change your mood." I loved this definition because it cuts across all manner of emotional circumstances.

An impulse to change my uncomfortable, unpleasant mood can take myriad forms from the self-destructive to the productive. And that is the aim here. What are the constructive distractions for our tribulations? A few beers or cocktails after a day in your salt mines is common and usually no big deal. If the routine includes passing out or cooking crystal meth, well, you've obviously entered maladaptive territory.

While a graduate student at Columbia University, training to be a clinical social worker, I did my first internship at the Lower East Side Service Center. This legendary clinic, devoted to serving persons with addictions and mental health issues, was in the Chinatown section of Lower Manhattan.

During our first week, the chief psychiatrist and our supervisor told us rookies during orientation, "Let's be clear. If you're not very nosy, you cannot be a therapist." My reaction was immediate – check! This has always been true for me. I have an insatiable curiosity about the lives of people – including myself. I'm a buttinsky.

It is all at once a wide-eyed fascination with nature and a desire to comprehend the existential and spiritual meaning of human life. After all, while doing this psychological training, I was simultaneously enrolled and thoroughly invested in a graduate program at Union Theological Seminary in theology. My nights were in the comedy clubs in New York City and my days were spent in classes and the clinic.

My Professor, Carol Meyer said that if I wanted to be a therapist it was essential, even an ethical imperative, to go through therapy myself. This was especially important given my interest to train in psychoanalysis. So, I set out to find my own analyst and met Dr. Janet Bachant, an eminent New York practitioner.

I found myself on her couch three mornings a week for about three years, plumbing the depths of my personal history. I learned a great deal, of course. Up to that point, my psychological self-assessment was pretty much confined to a few general observations such as irritability, free-floating fears like commitment, intimacy and being murdered. Pretty typical stuff, I believed.

Not only did I gain insight into my own neurotic character and disposition, it fueled my passion for the process of psychotherapy. I spent two more years after graduation studying at the Psychoanalytic Institute and I never turned back.

So, I have been shrinking people since the nineties, in a variety of settings, along with having been shrunk myself. I have a feel for the emotional complexities of human beings. I have years of experience with individual and family counseling, along with teaching and training others. Having spent my entire adult life studying, practicing and helping people use our human apparatus better, I am still only partially there myself.

But here we are, you and me; you the reader, who is wanting some insight into the issue at hand. You might be tapping your watch thinking, *"Okay get to it."*

## Now Back to You

Since this is a book, I can blather on with no risk for you. So, if this is worthwhile, because I do have an agenda, I'm asking you to rethink your work-misery conclusions. It is therapeutic to take in the larger context.

Let's go big with a macro view of your life and its real possibilities, seeing a picture of your life writ large, beyond the particulars of job, career, family life and very importantly, your real desires. Even if, by now, your true-life passions have been relegated to dim fantasies, indulge me. Let's make a brash suggestion: could it be that your conclusions about your gloomy job may be more psychologically involved than you think?

## A Fast Track Therapy Approach

Ever talk to someone who can't give you the Readers Digest version of their tale? You really only have about two minutes to chat with them at the printer but their story drones on with maddening, unnecessary details that is a full 10-minute script. It's usually the extraneous details that pad the story and you are trying to be patient but inside are screaming, "Get to the point! What she was driving and her choice of getting high-test gasoline is not necessary here! For the love of God bring it home!"

Okay, having just diverted you with an unnecessary paragraph myself, my gift is now a Reader's Digest synopsis of a valid psychological theory that can help speed you through on our way to your solution called Attribution Theory. It's an accessible, easily digestible psychological concept for understanding behavior and reactions to behavior.

Fritz Heider was a noted psychologist who was interested in developing a "common sense" psychological theory. Like all legendary shrinks, he was from Austria, the mother ship of psychoanalysis. Fritz was the one who espoused Attribution Theory, which "supposes that one attempts to understand the behavior of others by attributing feelings, beliefs, and intentions to them."[16]

The gist of the idea is that people intuitively explain what we observe, that we come to our own conclusion. Yeah, that's it. Well, almost. There is another layer below. In our explanations, Fritz differentiated between internal versus external explanations, or as he put it, "personal versus situational explanations". A personal, internal explanation attributes a situation to our own personality traits, strengths and vulnerabilities. External attribution is … well, you get it: something or someone else caused it.

We can each recall examples of internal cause. You know, when you shoot yourself in the foot? I moved a few times around the City during my comedy years before my wife, Sally and I, lived together. One year, I was living in Passaic, New Jersey, a tough urban suburb where I had a room in a house owned by a comedian's father who rented to comics.

I was broke and driving a hideous old AMC Matador when I decided to share an apartment on Long Island with my comedy

---

[16] Sanderson, Catherine (2010). Social Psychology. John Wiley & Sons. p. 112. ISBN 978-0-471-25026-5.

bud, Lou Dimaggio. He was helping me with the move. I was following his borrowed pickup truck loaded with my uncovered belongings on the highway, during a downpour.

A gust of wind suddenly lifted my bicycle from the truck bed and smashed it to the pavement. I then promptly ran over my own bike going 60 miles an hour. I rode this bike every day. It was my most valuable possession. When I took it to the bike shop, the owner told me somberly, "You destroyed every repairable part of the bike. It's totaled". I left the grim autopsy and knew immediately this was attributed to me.

In contrast, an external attribution is when you have been affected by an event or circumstance over which you had no control. For instance, when you get notice that your company is moving to China, you're hosed. And that's external attribution.

It can get complicated, of course. If you get notice from your boss that you've been canned, there's a pause. It might appear to be the boss' doing, and thus an external cause. But on reflection, you might recall that you did post some company secrets on Facebook. And then there was that time in the break room you got big laughs from everyone when you imitated how the boss walks like a duck.

Well then, that's your bad. Internal or external cause? You or them? Stick with this common sense psychological approach as we move on here. The legitimacy of your misery attribution might be tested and, hopefully, adjusted.

# CHAPTER 5

# Coping with Unintended Consequences

Given that the science is clear that unrelenting, chronic stress is what most plagues our health and has life threatening repercussions, how is your system doing? When the sore point of your life, the focus of your chronic stress is your job, what can you do about it? Have you settled for the unchangeable circumstances there?

Perhaps you are sucking up and enduring the pressure. Maybe you are also counting down the time until you can flee. When your world essentially revolves around your job and career, it's awful when it consistently disappoints you and corners you in a tedious and joyless position.

It seems to me that many of us have allowed ourselves to drift into our life predicament slowly, with too little notice of the aggravating factors. So, what are those ingredients? What is going on and who can we blame?

We will consider this by revisiting the attribution theory, that psychological approach to interpretation by our friend Fritz Heider. What's aggravating your misery index. Who and what is the culprit?

Let's start with external attribution and the factors you cannot control. The list of these is probably short and already well known to you. You can likely rattle off your complaints about your job spontaneously, even if the grievances are generalized. Often people will complain about the "bureaucracy" or "management". I've even heard some grouse about "political correctness." Those resentments all sound like situations over which you have no control – they are attributed externally by you.

## When It's Them!

Causes that are outside your control, are especially exasperating because they damper contentment with your job and career choice. Recall that curious predicament we observed earlier; many who are miserable at work still find meaning and even enjoyment in the actual work tasks they perform. So, it's stuff beyond these tasks, like the work environment.

The issue may be the actual physical setting, or more probably the social and relationship situation. In some cases, you might have input to make changes to the crummy, even hostile atmosphere, presuming you have the position and the respect of the decision makers. Is this possible? If so, I presume you would have already tried this approach without success. So, what are the factors outside of your control that are interfering with your fulfillment?

A laundry list would likely include company ownership whose regard for profits is without any balance for the well-being of the employees. "Sorry, the company is moving overseas. No choice. Stockholders come first. You understand." This is an infuriating experience, whether it's already come to pass or is hovering over everyone down the line like an anvil ready to drop. And, you can't even voice your feelings across the vast distance between you and some heartless suit in another city's high rise.

Maybe that rich, individual decision maker, living a thousand miles away, actually is feeling regret and sympathy for all of you scapegoats down the food chain. But he goes home to his family and sprawl, pity the sheep. Harsh I know, but isn't that the feeling you get watching helplessly from your position? It may be an unfair judgement of the power people, but it feels dreadful underneath.

Maybe your company is doing fine and dandy but your supervisor is an unhinged crackpot, either hostile or incoherent who you just happen to rub the wrong way. Maybe you've tried some relationship repair but the fix is in and you're the sap, the "fall guy".

Now in all honesty, can you discount with certainty that you are not the offender in this conflict? Are you sure it's not your fault? Any possibility you are the misery maker here? If it's them for sure, then you can attribute the torment to this external cause.

You're on the side of the attribution angels. Assuming it's them and not you, bear in mind that personality disorders are pretty common, and display a wide array of features. In fact, about one in ten people have a personality disorder, which is the clinical term for someone who is … well, insert your own rude term here,[17] but you get the picture. They're everywhere.

One study showed that roughly one in three clergy have a narcissistic personality disorder![18] Wow! Hey, I might be in that sample! Just as you are powerless to persuade the invisible stockholders about what you would like to see the company do for you, you can't control all the troubled personalities right around you every day.

It's not always obvious that someone has a screw loose. There's a term in therapy we use when someone has learned how to fake socially acceptable feelings. We call it the "as if" impression. The person does not feel compassion but is savvy enough to behave as if they do.

---

[17] Clark, L. A., Vanderbleek, E. N., Shapiro, J. L., Nuzum, H., Allen, X., Daly, E., … Ro, E. (2015). The Brave New World of Personality Disorder-Trait Specified: Effects of Additional Definitions on Coverage, Prevalence, and Comorbidity. Psychopathology Review, 2(1), 52–82. http://doi.org/10.5127/pr.036314

[18] R. Glenn Ball, et al. (2015). Frequency of Narcissistic Personality Disorder in Pastors: A Preliminary Study. http://www.darrellpuls.com/images/AACC_2015_Paper_NPD_in_Pastors.pdf

In extreme forms, you're dealing with a sociopath. Harvard psychologist, Martha Stout, has studied and written about sociopathology, the individual without a conscience, who lacks empathy for others and uses them for their own gain.[19] As she observes, the condition is not limited to the low-functioning criminals in prison; you know, murderers and other thugs, mugs and brutes. The actual frequency, she asserts, is a startling one in 25 people in the general population!

The high-functioning sociopath has mastered the "as if" approach to passing themselves off as a good citizen instead of the low life user-rat they are. So, if these scenarios describe your situation, then clearly you can attribute your struggles to variables beyond your control. We'll get to how you can contend with this stress later. Now, let's look at what might be attributable to you ... yes you, the embodiment of innocence, charisma, decency and rectitude!

## When It's You!

In situations where there are external causes for our stress and we feel helpless to change, the matter has some clarity. But while they are apparently beyond our control, we will see that we have a role to play in their making and undoing.

Since the end of World War II, amazing changes have altered the American lifestyle. But two trends, in particular,

---

19   Stout, M. (2005). The sociopath next door: The ruthless versus the rest of us. New York: Broadway Books.

have really disrupted social stability across the entire landscape. These two changes have far-reaching impact and contributed to destabilizing our lives, collectively and individually.

While these factors certainly appear to be situational, external causes for our predicament, a closer look reveals otherwise. The first is our constant moving, our ability to pack up, sell our houses and move to a new location. And the second is the tsunami of media and technology. These have brought about colossal changes in daily life. So, you ask, "Okay, so we move and use technology. How are these social factors attributed to my fault? This sounds like external attribution to me."

## On the Move

Let's start with America's amazing compulsion for relocation. The consequences of our mobility are profound to be sure and generally underestimated as well. Over the last six decades, Americans have moved at an astounding rate, by the tens of millions, every year.

In recent years, the number has grown to over 40 million relocations, one-third of which are beyond county and state[20].

Take a moment and think about that statistic – over 40 million people relocate every year! Stating the obvious, this pattern means that we routinely up and leave established relationships, along with familiarity of place and community. These losses are at the root of much psychosocial distress.

---

[20]    https://www.melissadata.com/enews/articles/0705b/1.htm

It's uncanny how little attribution we assign to the apparently ordinary act of packing up and leaving. Everyone has experienced leaving friends and family behind or being left by them when they move away. The sadness is palpable.

In my adult life, I have moved over a dozen times. I think I'm done, but make no guarantees. My reasons were typical, including career opportunity or for a relationship. Honestly, I cannot say they were always necessary. Yet in the moment, each seemed logical and rational.

Well, there was one exception. I was a senior in college in 1971 and the headline of the time was the "draft lottery". Before we went to the all-volunteer system, every male between the ages of 18 and 26 was deemed eligible to be drafted into the Army. They used a lottery system based on your date of birth. Your likelihood of being drafted was determined by where your birthdate came up in the draw.

The understanding was that anyone picked within the first 120 or so, of the 365 dates would be drafted. The Vietnam War was increasingly unpopular and most wanted to avoid it at all costs.

Guys were searching for creative ways to avoid being picked. There were only a few ways to dodge it. One was moving to Canada or some other country. Another was sweat it out getting a high number. And the last resort was being deemed unfit for service, the infamous Four-F designation. Clearly morale was at a low ebb.

The day of that first lottery, we were all chewing our nails in anticipation. We tried to find coverage of it on television in our dorm with no luck. Someone yelled down the hall, "Hey we got it here on the radio!" We bolted down in time to hear them pull birthdate number 15. There was a pause and with words I will never forget, I said to the guy next to me, "Who was the sucker who got number one?"

I'm sure you're ahead of me, it was September 14th, my bleeding birthdate! I called home and told my father whose response was a comforting "Well, at least you didn't have to listen to the whole program". So, I was going. And this was clearly external attribution!

## The Surprising Internal Attributions

Some people have the lucky fortune of being born and raised in an exciting place that offers seemingly limitless lifetime opportunities for work and joy. Yes, I'm talking to you, Hawaii and your paradise types.

Even if not some Garden of Eden setting, there are those who happily anticipate their own independent life right where they were born. Maybe they were in line to take over a beloved family business or had a passion for a career unique to their home town. Talking to you, young actors raised in Hollywood and aspiring tug boat captains from Hoboken.

For most, however, we grew up anticipating and fantasizing life somewhere new, somewhere else, and as soon as possible.

Moving away from home can be a long-held dream, like George Bailey in *It's a Wonderful Life*. Frequently though, it's prompted by a job opportunity or a relationship as in my case.

Our moving doesn't stop with just that first move from our childhood home. Like me, most of us are serial movers, relocating multiple times over the course of our lives. Americans between the ages of 20 and 35 move once every three years. We are free to go; free to run to; or flee from wherever. Good for us in America!

A seemingly minor, but consequential feature of this pattern, is that we usually make the journey alone or with precious few others. We're not the traveling clans of other cultures, where everyone from grandfathers, teens, and infants all load up and go together.

Curiously, we would be better off if we did move like the clan travelers – bringing our whole support system with us. Not so with us. We move solo or with the few in our mini unit, spouse-partner and kids. Why not? This is our treasured American individualistic spirit at work. We're outta here!

Packing up and getting away is an itch wanting to be scratched from early in our lives. And like George Bailey, many of us were infatuated with adventures imagined elsewhere. We soak up a steady stream of vivid, colorful images in media that promise a better life somewhere else.

Wherever you have chosen to go, it is surprising how casually we make our moves and how little we seem to fathom the profound psychological toll moving takes on us. In most cases, there is understandable excitement and thrill to reach our destination.

It seems, however, that we miscalculate the cost of losing so many well-established, diverse personal relationships. And worse, we seem generally oblivious to the difficulty of recreating adequate successors to those left behind.

Now honestly, there is no fantasizing about this particular matter for some people. Countless leavers do so motivated as much for the leaving as for the going. If you are escaping a dysfunctional, toxic relationship environment, the leaving can be a life-saving experience. In most cases though, leaving for opportunity comes with sadness for relationships left behind.

Are you leaving siblings, parents and close friends? Are there uncles, aunts, cousins and children to be missed? It's no small matter to lose their daily presence. But, who can possibly take their place? Not to mention, how in the world do you go about making such relationships begin and take root? There is unambiguous evidence correlating inadequate social connections with depression, anxiety and their attendant, inevitable health consequences.

When Glenn Sparks and I wrote our book, *Refrigerator Rights*, we documented this systemic problem of social isolation in America brought about, in no small part, to moving. Often, we would be asked by interviewers what people could do to make new connections. They would prompt us to offer concrete solutions for getting new friends who could fill in for the relationships we left behind.

I admit to reacting with surprised frustration at this – what seemed to me – absurd question. Glenn was amused when I would privately snap and say, "What do you need from us? Should we come to your house and walk you over to the next-door neighbor and introduce you? Hi, Mr. & Mrs. Baxter, this is Rita and Fred from next door and they are in need of establishing closer relationships with others nearby. Are you game for them to get connected? May we come in?" Evidently my snarky suggestion was never received as constructive.

Be that as it may, the issue remains as urgent as ever. Moving away from well-formed relationships, especially extended family who have loved, supported and mentored us, has huge consequences for coping with our life trials. How easy it is to dismiss the power of love that surrounded you from the people in your life, whether blood relatives, work and neighbor friends and others in the community that know you and embraced you.

The pertinent attribution issue in this case is a call to reflect on our moving patterns and the hefty psychological price you have paid. So, digesting this, what now for you? Are your roots planted deep where you are presently or are you living in a vase? Just how much of your angst and chronic stress is really attributable to your own choices? What part have you played in subtle and systematic winnowing down of your social support system by moving and failing to reconnect? How socially isolated are you?

## A Witless New World

Piling onto the dire, systemic psychological consequences of repeated relocation, a compounding variable is the new reality of technology and media. The mantra for our work on social isolation has been both moving and media, as the perfect storm for our ailing condition.

It's not lost on anyone, that technology, in its varied forms, has utterly transformed all facets of daily life for everyone. Whether someone is fully engaged in technology or a disengaged luddite, all forms of communication, information and entertainment are now delivered electronically.

Especially relevant for our discussion is this combination of relocation and technology that perpetuates disconnection and loss of critical relationships. This transformation is now a half-century in the making and its consequences are being fully felt.

This all leads to the issue at hand – why are so many of us in our time and place, so ill-at-ease, depressed, anxious and on the edges of emotional misery? If we accept that human frailty is our condition, what are the variables – controlled or otherwise – that so often puncture our moment-to-moment happiness?

I will offer that these twin habits of moving and media have clearly made matters worse for us. Shedding our long-established relationships that have been built over years, for some misguided and myopic pipe-dream about the better life somewhere else, is sometimes a disappointment and even a fool's errand.

Even when deciding to change places, what then? We allow ourselves to be consumed by technology and media hindering formation of new connections. We wind up with a weak network of casual contacts with new neighbors, co-workers and of course, our five hundred close Facebook friends. We trade intimacy for familiarity.

These accepted habits have played to the weakest parts of our brain. Moving, combined with media, fuels social isolation to the max and is, quite honestly, a lifestyle for suckers.

In their comprehensive analysis of the current state of media technology and its impact on our psychological and physical health, researchers Gazzaley and Rosen make a riveting case for how technology is impoverishing and depleting our functioning.[21]

They document in detail that we simply do not have the ability to perform at full capacity while engaging in active use of media technology. Multitasking is now a fantasy and a debunked myth. We are adept at rapidly switching from task to task, diminishing the focus and engagement of each briefly visited focal point.

What we are doing, in fact, is simply distracting ourselves away from whatever feels discomforting, cognitively and emotionally. An impulse to change our mood.

---

[21] Gazzaley, A., Rosen, Larry (2016) The Distracted Mind: Ancient Brains in a High-Tech World. MIT Press.

Neil Postman's prescient book, *Amusing Ourselves to Death* (1985)[22] offered a compelling insight into modern life in comparing two of the memorable novels of the last century – Aldous Huxley's *Brave New World*, published in 1932[23] and George Orwell's *1984*, published in 1949[24].

Each gave a vision for a totalitarian society that was chilling indeed. The Orwell fantasy was a chilling account of a central government authority that was always watching and monitoring our activities and compliance. The term "Big Brother" entered our vocabulary, a caution against the tyranny of obsessive, intrusive authority. It has come to be true, especially in repressive regimes around the globe, where 'Big Brother' controls through violence and torture.

In contrast, Huxley imagined controlling the population through drugs and pleasure, which has proven perhaps more prophetic in that we are now addicted to our amusements: social media, gaming and other distractions.

Every hour we are looking at a screen, is an hour not looking at a face. Every minute engaged in detached media, is a minute not focusing on our goals and actions to move toward them. An enormous amount of our time is diverted to amusements and away from the actions that will actually improve the quality of our lives.

---

[22]  Neal Postman, Amusing Ourselves to Death: Public Discourse in the Age of Show Business (1985)

[23]  Aldous Huxley, *Brave New World* (1931)

[24]  George Orwell, *1984* (1949)

Ours is a life of perpetual interruption and distraction. I remember the impact of someone's observation about my hobby of photography. He said, "Don't replace actually having an experience because you are too busy photographing and documenting the experience to look at later." He was right. Did I really absorb the view of the vista with my own eyes or mostly through the lens?

Okay, so let's digest this matter. Hopefully, you've done some soul-searching about your relocation history and the choices you made that involved leaving relationships and failing to reconnect. How much of the analysis of technology use relates to you and the circle of people around you?

You know the cliché; a family sits around the dinner table each looking at their cellphones. It's ongoing conversation with each other that is being replaced by passive engagement in media. No one says any of this is easy, and the price of moving has already been paid. Looking back, you can think about that cost analysis of opportunity versus your losses.

And now, going forward you can also calculate how much your personal, possibly addictive habits of tech engagement have served as an unintended obstacle to opportunities for new connections. Has your social world been reduced to your significant other and a couple of kids? Is your extended social world a mixture of work acquaintances, some neighbors and a few other friends?

It's clear that while it is easy to look at our struggles being externally caused, we have played more of a role than we may have imagined. How much of my overall life discontentment is actually my bad? Think about your life choices and how they relate to the effects of your own moving and media habits. How have you tried to balance your frenetic lifestyle? Let's look at another way to frame your life situation.

## The Control Problem

Kids don't control their lives. Even if after a certain age, they strut around as if they have it all going on. It's managed by others who, hopefully, are merciful people who love and protect them. That story has a million variations and some of you know exactly what this has meant.

Growing up under the authority of the stable and kindhearted is nothing less than the expectation in human families. Like most children growing up in a strict family, I never had illusions that I had much of any say over what was happening in my life. My wiggle room was confined to operating within the narrow boundaries available in the house, at school and in church. My only area of personal empowerment was my limited free time.

Psychologist Julian Rotter observed that individuals have a varying sense of their "locus of control".[25] Along the continuum, we tend toward having either an internal or an external locus of

---

[25]  Julian Rotter, *Locus of Control*

control. Do we feel a sense of mastery over our lives or are we essentially at the mercy of external forces? It can be applied, of course, not only to us individually, but can also describe groups and entire societies.

When this dynamic is writ large, we can see whole populations lean toward external locus of control when suffering under social and political oppression by repressive regimes. Here, there is little illusion about personal control, beyond the most urgent activities for survival. It's difficult to imagine the impact of these situations that transfer across generations of the oppressed.

At the mercy of external forces, coping is the matter of the moment. In situations of natural catastrophe, there is at least the shred of hope that the situation will pass and control can be restored. Repression is a different story entirely and it is the scourge of human existence.

In contrast to these dire illustrations, we come then to understand that our own way of life is characterized more by an internal locus of control. At least this is our expectation. Personal dominion over my life is a central, psychological feature of the American promise.

We are task-oriented, accomplishment-focused, and presume to solve problems ourselves. In popular psychology, whether in forms of cognitive behavioral approaches, self-help or motivation, the foundation is mastery. We presume we can be and should be in total charge of our life and actions.

True enough with the rational understanding that this is not always the situation. Because sometimes it's fuzzy. Sometimes constraints and demands disrupt our desires.

Clearing the air here, let's start with the obvious question. Which part of your life gives you the most fertile opportunity for command and control? It's certainly possible that you rule at work. You may be swimming along with the balanced life and the job is gratifying and still holds your interest, passion and career dreams. Okay, maybe you're the boss. What about the people around you and those working under you? How are they doing and how aware are you about how they are doing?

So, let's wrap up this idea. If you can accept the fact that you actually have a say in your lifestyle choices when it comes to the two big social forces of place stability and use of technology, the locus of your control may be more internal than you assume. You may, in fact, have to accept that the overall life situation in which you find yourself is the result of your own choices. We're talking then about internal attribution more than what you might have realized.

# CHAPTER 6

# Central Life Interest

We can't talk about the American labor force and the workplace in the abstract as if it's one big thing. If the goal is to give counsel across the board, to people who suffer stress with their job, how can we think about it?

Not long ago, my wife Sally reminded me of the concept she studied in her doctoral program, called "central life interest." This term, well known in the academic literature, has been around for decades. In this context, it immediately caught my attention.

Central life interest was used by sociologist Robert Dubin, in the mid 1950's during his research on urban workers and their loyalties. And although the term has a rich history in industrial psychology, it is also a useful phrase to clarify anyone's frame of mind toward their life and work. And it may be a useful concept for our purposes.

Central life interest refers to – as it says – the part of my life that most attracts my interest; that facet of life that gives me the most joy. When considering how to apportion my energies into different parts of daily life, what is the activity that best captures me? What would I rather be doing, instead of attending to almost every other demand in my life?

It's a simple exercise and a useful reflection. We each juggle our life's responsibilities but can readily acknowledge which activity gives us our greatest joy. It helps me to identify the activities where my passions are stirred. Ascertaining this specific locus of gratification is essential to admit for our emotional well-being.

This tale is part of my own family history. It's fair to observe that there was a signature shift from the life perspective of our greatest generation parents and us sixties children.

My father's service during World War II was truly heroic. A gunner on a B26 Marauder light bomber, his crew flew 48 dangerous missions in Europe. Here was a kid from a small, working class family in New Jersey, who suddenly found himself in this harrowing reality. Like so many of that aptly named "Greatest Generation" he served, he was highly decorated and survived.

Marrying my mother right after the war, they built a family of eight kids, four boys and four girls. One brother Robert, died as a baby and the rest of us grew up and went out into the world. During these years, Dad worked for the Brooklyn Union Gas Company. His expertise was heating and air-conditioning and he spent his days going in and out of houses and businesses, installing and fixing their gas utilities.

For the first 10 years, they lived in Brooklyn and then bought a house on Long Island. Getting up before dawn, he commuted with a couple of other guys through the dense Long Island traffic to Brooklyn. He worked loyally with the company for 40 years. I spent a couple of my summers home from college making that same trek to work for the gas company and got a feel for his routine.

Looking back, I marvel at his quiet devotion to all his life duties and responsibilities and don't remember him ever missing a day. And I never heard him complain about his job either. Perhaps he kept any work problems confined to conversations with my mother. While the weekly grind was surely exhausting, he was always fully engaged with the family. In fact, it was his family that was his central life interest.

Things changed vividly for their kids. I don't know how this was inculcated so strongly, but my parents were insistent that each of us go to college. Education was their value esteemed above all others except, of course, for our faith. Almost every one of my neighbors and classmates in school were from blue-collar families with parents pushing us to succeed academically.

Education was essential and not for debate in our home. I was antsy and distracted and consequently got only modest grades, but it was never an option to not get a degree after high school. My siblings, better students than me, all went on to receive a bachelor's degree and most graduate degrees as well. My journey accruing five graduate degrees was clearly psychological compensation for earlier under achievement. So, in one generation, we made a collar change from blue to white.

Every one of my siblings and their spouses and continuing on to the next generation, can all be described as reflecting a shift of our central life interest to our careers. We have all been aspirational, professional seekers in our chosen professions. Our jobs have been our careers and our careers have been our life's primary focus. Despite the caution against this kind of thinking, I'd have to say that for many of us, our career or job, became fused with our identity.

This was certainly true for me, especially since I never had children of my own. By the time I became a stepparent, Tamara and Tom were teenagers, beyond the stage where my daily lifestyle was radically altered. My central life interest has always been my career, whether as a comedian, teacher, therapist and even minister. My life has always been tied tightly to my job of the moment.

When I first began shifting from standup comedy to corporate entertainment and public speaking, the phrase most often used to describe me was an authority on "life balance." I was there to offer advice on how to manage career passion with a gratifying family life at home. I was getting hired to speak on this issue because, evidently, it was a need felt in companies and organizations that people were not balancing very well.

The motivation for the companies hiring me was primarily to address the problem of worker health and motivation. A big part of the appeal was that my presentation included standup comedy which the audiences really enjoyed. The comedy helped them absorb my serious message and it worked.

From management's point of view, addressing worker stress was not just about doing a good turn for their employees. It had real tangible and measurable consequences on performance and, of course, profit. So, I was among the top-tier speakers on life balance. Before too long, however, the term seemed to be played, if not passé. This was around the time of the recession and the focus shifted to the urgency of the economic challenges in a recession.

What advice do we give in light of this situation? One obvious answer to the complaining worker is to find a new job. Okay, that can work. And I'm sure there are many who could testify that this was exactly what they needed to do and that all is well for the moment. Of course, not everyone has this luxury or flexibility. For many, there are limited options.

Professionals can revise their resume and find a less toxic situation. For others, it's back to the want ads. But will the new school, plant, hospital or office be better? It's a dicey situation when even considering making a job change. On top of the present angst I'm enduring each day, I now have to suck it up and face the appalling chore of looking and worse, getting a new, better job. Just the thought can make us wobbly. But the present is not acceptable so now it's time to gear up and get ready to – God help me, interview!

Since the scary nadir of the recession, some things have changed. While there has been some recovery in business and profits, matters have not apparently recovered when it comes to worker contentment and enthusiasm. There is a general worry about the future of the country.

News analysis raises widespread anxiety about the consequences of national economic security, globalization and even uncertainty about social stability. While we have certainly been through phases of such angst before, there is increased stress on everyone worrying about the reliability of their job and ability to earn a living. Not everyone is a nervous wreck. But those who appear calm may well be repressing or displacing their fears. This means we are revisiting the issue of managing our mood.

In recent years, the requests for my presentation have overwhelmingly been about coping with stress. I'm among many well-established corporate speakers who come before audiences of harried professionals to offer insights and strategies for alleviating their stress. Most of my peers have specific definable strategies, based on the best psychological science available, to have the audience walk away feeling confident and empowered that they can improve their state of mind.

The strategies are aimed at each person individually, for them to take in and take home the practices that we know can offer relief. I know from observation that these presentations are powerful, even electrifying, and audience members walk out enthused and confident.

How long the effect lasts is unknown. I'm not aware of any widespread change in the psychological well-being of workers who have been to a motivational speech. Could it be that increasing numbers of people have just given up expecting that their job is going to bring them the gratification they had hoped?

My father's generation predates the emergence of this great stress crisis. The Brooklyn Union Gas Company remained the same institution for the four decades he worked there. His salary was secure even if raises were paltry and his beloved pension remained intact years after he was gone. However, since his retirement, the company has been bought out and the younger workers have faced the changes coming about with the new order of ownership and management.

When we reflect on the divide in the population that has fueled the economic and political tensions of the past few decades, we have a tendency to attribute the schisms to the divide in education and economic prosperity. And fair enough, these divides are real. But, looking at this from the perspective of our central life interest, it seems that each distinct segment of the population is equally disillusioned with their jobs.

Whether you are a devoted worker to a job like my father or a dedicated career professional like his kids, we are joined together, being hosed by the systemic changes outside our control. A factory worker in Indiana who learns the company is moving out of the country, is every bit as furious with his state as the teacher enduring helicopter politicians micromanaging their third-grade classroom.

Where does this leave us when, regardless of where we are in our job world, we have little power or influence to change the game? The challenge of coping is, therefore, anecdotally tied to each situation. The stability and joy of your work life may be moving along swimmingly. And if you're blessed enough to have your personal life also rich and fulfilling, there's obviously much to be thankful for at the moment.

But for those confronting uncertainty and pressure in your work world, again whether job or career, you are confronted with a choice. If you can't change your work, you certainly have capacity to address the joy of your home life. Even if your personal relationships, marriage, children and extended family are chaotic, you do have the capacity to assume more control in this domain. If you can't fix everything, fix what you can fix.

And this brings us back to the theme of this chapter about defining your central life interest. Whether your professional career dreams have buckled or the job you have is showing signs of crumbling, finding a new path to earn a living may not be easy, but it is certainly possible. It also circles us back to the notion of life balance.

When you're balancing on the fulcrum of a seesaw, you know that staying upright involves the subtleties of shifting your weight. This is not to suggest that you abandon the joy of your job or career. But shifting your balance from work during periods of instability, to the joy that can be captured in your personal life, is the goal of coping.

Odd as it may sound, a surprising number of people resist admitting that they would rather be spending their days doing something other than what they do. Is it guilt? Some of it, sure. Too many of those I see in therapy fiercely resist allowing themselves the freedom to identify their central life interest. The endeavor gets confused with notions of obligation and demands. But clarifying our central life interest is the starting place for change.

It is an idea that enables us to see ourselves clearly, in contrast to being at the mercy of how others see us. Moving your central life interest to the relationships outside of work, is the starting point.

# CHAPTER 7

# Recalibrating, A Biopsychosocial Highway

It's predictable that self-help would prosper in our culture. It offers fast change that will last your lifetime. At least that's in the brochure and on the website. Our hunger for information and insight is ravenous. In fact, it's a biological, evolutionary drive for all of us.

My encounters with people give me the sense that many of their insights about life come from a combination gleaned from others. Some of these others are people they know, as well as added input from professionals.

The challenge, of course, is synthesizing this avalanche of input which sometimes conflict with each other. Some become devotee disciples of one chosen perspective. Seeing the world through their lens – or is it prism – we fuse the values taken from our ethic roots with the appealing ideas we absorb as we step out into the world.

If helpful insights are now readily available through media, does this not just add to the confusion? Can the cacophony of distracting ideas overwhelm our ability to sort the counsel and integrate?

I tend to find credibility in many of the success systems offered through promotion and advertising. Tony Robbins, Stephen Covey, Suze Orman, Wayne Dyer, Zig Ziglar, even Mr. T, all give motivational speeches. They've all gotten rich and when you hear their advice, it makes good sense. I come away from these thinking, "Yeah I already knew that. Thanks for reminding me. I'll recommit to trying again."

## Self-Help: meh

My transition to public, corporate speaking was from standup comedy in the nightclubs. Tired of the rough and raucous nightclub environment, my managers helped me transition to the corporate speaking tour, first as a comic and eventually as a comic with a message.

My message was taken from my book, *Refrigerator Rights*, about the health effects of social isolation. Mixed with standup routines, it brought me lots of opportunities to speak. And since I was comfortable on stage in front of large audiences, there was demand for me. I was delivering 30 to 40 keynotes a year. Well, good for me. Except I've always felt somewhat self-conscious for not having a comparable program of applicable advice.

As diverse as we claim to be in America, there is a certain homogeneity to the influences that shape us. Our meaning tends to organize around some predominant, predictable ideas. We are encouraged to be patriotic and loyal to the founding principles of our country. We are encouraged to bond in the communities where we live and traditionally in gatherings of religious faith, as well.

While structures of the latter organizing, principle are in steep decline, the foundations of the Judeo-Christian religious traditions still penetrate the national zeitgeist. I was certainly fed a hefty diet of Roman Catholicism throughout my childhood. Talk about lofty ideas struggling to be grasped!

Both the clever and the dense among us share the same desire to be happy most of the time every day. For this to happen, the best chance includes having a lifestyle that is well balanced. Remember Freud's advice that "Love and work are the cornerstones to our humanness"? Finding this balance, means shifting your central life interest away from a narrow focus on job and career. You can find great fulfillment in work. I certainly do. But it alone cannot carry the weight of our emotional needs.

Fulfillment is found principally in love and that means your relationships. If you have too few close connections, you'll never withstand the burden of your isolation. And if too many of the relationships you do have are contentious and disagreeable, the stress will shorten your already emotionally exhausting life. So, for the love of God, isn't it time to recalibrate?

Someone recently posted on Facebook an amusing take on life: "The three stages of life: Birth, What the hell is this, Death." For all of us in the middle stage, we go day-to-day making it work – somehow.

We creatures of the fat frontal cortex wrestle with our yearnings and our reality. Unless you are one whose life is devoted to existential reflection 24/7, the rest carry on with the mundane pursuit of coping. We manage the problems and conflicts we already face and are alert for the unexpected addition to the daily agenda.

Family matters and work matters are under control, even if distressing. But then, we have the repressed worries about the unforeseen crisis, large or small. Let's face it, being a human being is simply an extraordinary experience! Assisting us along the way is the collective wisdom of the ages. It has everything we need to find our way.

Sifting through the ocean of sage thought, however, can overwhelm us. But it is there for everyone. Classical philosophy, new age spirituality, popular psychology and psychotherapy, sacred texts, sermons, mindfulness and meditation or just the counsel of your nearby elders – it is all available at the buffet, live and online.

You'll recall that high-minded term from health science, known as the biopsychosocial approach. In light of our review of factors relevant to your misery dilemma, let's break it down and talk about the implications for each part of this approach. Having refreshed our understanding about the destructive, yet subtle power of chronic stress, let's start with your body.

## The BIO

Awareness about the need to take care of our physical health has long been valued, of course. But the rise of passionate devotion to physical fitness and body shaping is a more recent phenomenon. This trend is also tied to the focus on healthy eating.

It was probably the Generation X teens and adults who ushered this into the popular culture. Baby boomers joined the trend and a billion-dollar industry is thriving, answering the demand for body wellness. It's certainly an admirable craze that's reasonably promoted and supported in the marketplace and through policy. But it is a somewhat recent trend.

My parents and everyone I knew of their generation in my family, and I'll even go back and include my grandparents, all had a similar lifestyle. Their jobs, roles, diet and other habits were all predictable and consistent. I make this observation to then say, that I never in my entire life, ever saw anyone of them formally exercise. The only time anyone of them ever did, was likely the men in the military.

The whole time I was growing up, I never once heard any of the adults in my life use the words "abs, glutes, pecs or reps". Complimenting someone on their abs could easily get you kicked in your glutes. Health and exercise was not part of a lot of conversations. In my world, it was more common to hear an adult say "Got a light?"

Sadly, I've carried on this tradition. With the exception of push-ups, pull-ups and jumping jacks in basic training where, by the way, I also was a smoker, I have never cultivated the discipline of exercise. It's terrible. I know and I confess this appalling fact. The motivation to regularly and formally work out has never really overtaken me.

With no credit to myself, I've never really struggled with a lack of energy or severe weight problems. After my heart attack, I attended a few weeks of rehab sessions where I walked on the treadmill. And over this past year, I've tried to be consistent about walking a mile every day, although honestly, I probably average once a week.

Yes, I'm self-conscious about this shameful declaration and in no way am I advocating anyone follow my pathetic example. I can only recommit to a lifestyle change, or at least a tweak, where a term like 'reps' becomes part of my lexicon.

Why drift off topic with this observation and disclosure? Surely, health science affirms that exercise is a critical strategy for coping with stress. A growing number of companies encourage their workers to engage in exercise and other healthy activities. These wellness programs are designed to serve the mutual interests of the organization and the workers.

Healthy workers miss fewer days and stay fit for their tasks. While these initiatives are laudable, it doesn't seem that it's having a measurable impact on worker mood and motivation. A treadmill at the office does not by itself compensate for the stress being felt by the job's demands and pressures.

A sobering new study by the American Heart Association showed a disturbing correlation between exercising while you are angry and an increased risk of having a fatal heart attack![26] This raises the intriguing prospect that some workers, so frustrated with their job, might be trying to "work off" their anger by vigorously exercising. Well, that needs to be reconsidered!

Physical exercise is certainly an important prescription for coping with stress. The most immediate symptoms of stress discomfort, however, are felt psychologically. The range of emotions include frustration, anger, even rage. But these feelings are all necessarily repressed for fear of the consequences of acting out. It's worth keeping in mind, however, that the physiological impact of chronic stress most certainly develops eventually.

We all have had roles in this drama; the urge to lash out is pushed down, given the calculation that the consequences could

---

[26] American Heart Association Circulation. "Physical Activity and Anger or Emotional Upset as Triggers of Acute Myocardial Infarction" (2016) Smyth, et al.

only get worse. Well it's now clear that running and weightlifting are ill-advised when you're furious.

The lesson here is dedication with moderation. Taking care of ourselves physically, with appropriate exercise and a good diet, is obviously correlated with lowering stress. It is not difficult at all to learn everything you need about this topic with a little research.

Seriously, information abounds online and through friends. I've sometimes mentioned sarcastically to people seeking help that they might try just looking around at some others. Pick out someone who seems to be hale and hearty and imitate them. Comedian Mike Reynolds had a bit in his act about getting healthy. So, he went to the supermarket and followed around someone who looked very healthy and then stole their cart.

We both know what we should do so why aren't we doing it? What's clear, is that the strategy for alleviating the eroding effects of the chronic stress slow cooker, is to find ways to relieve your body of its encroaching damage.

Bio recalibrating means tying together the insights of health science about the silent, unconscious damage chronic stress is doing to you, with some bio triage to control (or at least moderate) the harm.

We all have those friends who run marathons and participate in Ironman competitions. I'm happy to hang around onshore and clap for them when they come out of the water. But I'll be fully dressed and drinking coffee. Well, wait. Out of respect, I'll probably just have water…you know…hydrating. The treatment plan for your body is to counteract stress with exercise and diet, but it's not just this alone.

## The PSYCHO

Apologies to all those professional success gurus out there, the positive thinkers and the "you can do it" apostles. The chapter on our psychological design, purposely used that word – fragile. I understand the pushback against this, as it seems like an accusation that I think you are weak. Well okay, I acknowledge that you probably have a Spartan aura about you. You are strong, perhaps even savage in your presentation. But of course, I know better. That's just your packaging.

No human being is immune to self-doubt and the fear of vulnerability, even if not actually feeling vulnerable. This is not to say that some have cultivated a petrified persona, that reveals no inkling of insecurity. And they might even assert that they are fine with this and follow it by turning their head and spitting.

Be that as it may, as observed earlier – emotional well-being, when working in concert with our physical health, allows for introspection, transparency and, yes, vulnerability. This does not mean becoming a wimpy poodle, particularly when out in public among strangers. But it does advocate for an openness with the intimates in your life, to process aloud what moves and troubles you. If your intimate relationships are either too complicated or worse, absent, it's an act of strength to seek help and counseling.

Going to a shrink, a trusted clergy or even a wise mentoring friend is how human beings process when we feel stuck. In the absence of such a healthy approach, we always have those reliable companions: denial and repression. As you can guess, I'm no fan of either of these regressive defenses. It's hard to determine when 'sucking it up' crosses over to just bottling up your emotions.

When you fall into this pattern, as sure as Freud had a beard, your body will rebel and you will get sick. First, you get emotionally sick and eventually, physically sick.

What's a strategy here? If your internal engine has already started leaking into a depression or idling too high in anxiety, what do you do? Recall that if physical exercise can help stem the tide of physiological damage from stress, what helps me with what's going on between my ears and in my gut?

Well, what do you think? Hello McFly! You need to get professional help in therapy. That's one tried and tested approach. It is not weakness. In fact, it's a character strength to get help. And most therapists have an office setup where you can sneak in and skulk back out with healing in between. And there is something else.

The past two decades has witnessed emerging research strongly supporting practices that fall under the generic term of "mindfulness." I recognize that this word has no clear descriptive use. My guess is that suggesting mindfulness would be met with the response, "What's that?" in virtually every instance. And it doesn't help when you try to clarify by using the term "meditation." This too, is laden with images of some kind of Eastern religious esoterica and often prompts a flat-out rejection and perhaps a suspicion that I, myself, am probably going to hell.

Yes, the approach does have an image problem. I have been trying to persuade police officers to incorporate brief mediation exercises into their work day. I get eye rolls of course, but they usually hear me out with my pitch. And more recently, I have used the subversive tactic of convincing their spouses of the benefits. It remains to be seen, but I know it's effective.

So ... what to do? I don't have a suggestion for a better term than mindfulness practices, but feel compelled to push on with the recommendation. The science is undeniable that resting your galloping brain for even brief periods each day has a remarkable, sustained impact on lowering stress. It lowers your blood pressure, slows your heart rate and allows your mind to process matters more clearly. And those bio effects obviously settle your psyche simultaneously.

## The SOCIAL

The social element of the approach is sometimes murky, because it seems essentially an external variable I cannot control. But not necessarily so. The reason the biopsychosocial approach is so effective is because it gives a map for delving into the root of someone's presenting problem from their bod through their mind and into their life. This isn't just psychobabble. It's a really elegant, intellectual approach that works in helping people. And the social piece is really enlightening.

The best example I can recall was when I was training as a clinical social worker in New York and Sally was an elementary school principal. We would discuss the issues of the day for each of us and I can remember a vivid illustration of this diagnostic approach coming from schools. It's a simple way to look at it.

A child is acting out in school, misbehaving and being defiant. The frustrated teacher referring the child to the office, inquires whether there is some physical or health issue at work. Clarifying that there are no underlying physical problems, it might appear on the surface that presenting problem begins and ends with the disruptive behavior, a psychologically challenged student.

But, with a little more inquiry by the counselor, it's discovered that this child goes home to a chaotic family of neglect, disorder and perhaps even violence. Too overwhelmed and timid to act out there, his behavior at school becomes a signal that something else is going on. In the words of the clinician, the home is the real patient. The kid's behavior is just the symptom. Ruling out the bio and even reframing the psycho, you get to the real presenting problem – the sick environment in his house!

Returning to the premise of calculating, or recalculating that attribution matter, take a moment and think about which part of your life is actually disappointing you more. Even if the job is a principal irritation, what is the case at home after work?

It is my observation and my ardent belief that an overwhelming number of people miserable at work have failed to acknowledge the absence of the social support system necessary to adequately function. It's no big stretch to see yourself in this illustration. At the risk of making a comparison that might well be too facile, what really is the root problem? Might it be the job exclusively? Sure.

I tend to be skeptical, however, that in many situations, the struggling worker is like that disruptive kid. And whereas a nine-year-old only knows how to act out with defiance and rude behavior at school, outside the house, adults have a much more sophisticated arsenal at our disposal. We can displace work pressures to other relationships. We can repress our helpless rage and quietly eat through the lining of our stomach.

Let's consider your home life. It's been made vividly clear that our collective habits of moving away, or perhaps better stated abandoning familiar relationships and places, has terrible consequences. And the natural human urge to reconnect is profoundly compromised by diverting our attention to technology and media. So, under the best circumstances, the American home life is in some real distress. We rely on too few relationships for our emotional balance. And the few we have, namely our significant other, often become overheated and tense.

A truth in basic Psychology 101 is that one person cannot handle the whole emotional load of you. And you have no business presuming that you can be the emotional fulfillment of another individual. Nothing squeezes intimate relationships, which started with beautiful passion, more predictably than being an isolated couple, dependent on each other and your children for your fulfillment.

I'm convinced after many years as a shrink, that this is a significant underlying, underappreciated cause of divorce. We appear to be clueless about how to repopulate a healthy family life. Are you really sure that this is not what's really making you miserable? Taking stock of your social world, means a candid evaluation of who and how many are around you. Is it only you, your spouse and your kids? You do know what a full family of relationships looks like. Where are the nieces and nephews, cousins, aunts, uncles and grandparents?

As psychologically sophisticated as we are, we have marginalized as an expendable luxury, the necessity for extended family.

My advice is this: if you really want to fix your emotional interior, address what's absent in your life exterior. Fix the outside, to change the inside. If you're alone and cut off, well by gum, you'll adapt to that reality and try to soldier on. But know this: study after study affirms that isolation and loneliness don't just harm us, they lower our mood.

In the blunt words of the 75-year Harvard happiness study: 'loneliness kills.' Rethink your attribution calculation and do the assessment of your life outside work. When that's fixed and fulfilling, whatever is left on your misery plate can actually be attributed, externally, to your lousy job. But even then, you will have others you can come home to and share the complaints with support, compassion and even laughter.

Assuming you have been inundated with advice, both expert and non-professional, from Dr. Phil and your grandmother, what elevates us above the noise, to grasp an approach to living that will, if not raise us up to real joy? What will magnify and sustain high spirits. Let's finally turn to some ideas about life sublime.

# CHAPTER 8

# Your People Are My People

Having tortured you with plenty of psychobabble, let's talk turkey about what can help relieve your work and life miseries. If you haven't already guessed, the misery culprit is more likely about an anemic social world. Specifically, you just don't have enough life outside of work. You have familiarity with many, but emotional closeness with few. You have to fix this.

This thought may cause a gag response, thinking you can't add another thing to your life. But you see, it's a classic balance issue. Your central life interest has drifted into your career by default because you don't feel you have the option to put your interests elsewhere. Like millions of other Americans, you are trying to find contentment with your job that, even if the work itself continues to be satisfying, is leaving you frustrated and emotionally empty.

If this resonates with you, let's talk about a strategy for fixing it. For starters, who occupies your world outside of work? Who is in your home? Is it you and a typical micro unit of spouse and some kids? Are you alone? Is it complicated with displaced adult children who juggle visitation complications with in-laws? Who can come into the house or apartment without feeling like a guest? If your social world consists of only a few people, it's just not enough.

And remember, this is well-researched health science, not just a feel good fuzzy suggestion. It's your life – body and soul. It's no easy task getting emotionally close to others outside your current little intimacy pod. Expanding it takes time and intention. It takes a lot of time and a lot of intention.

The loss of your connections is most frequently due to either moving away or being left by others when they relocate. But, there is that other intrusive variable: gadget-world. We give hours to media and substituting real live friends with online friendships. How's this working?

Yes, there are benefits to these amazing technologies. My family is scattered all over God's green earth and Facebook is an amazing gift for staying connected to them. I see them grow, graduate, get married and have kids right online! In this regard, it's miraculous. But, losing hours every day to this screen world is causing you and your family to drift farther away from the connections needed for a healthy human life.

Here is something curious to chew on: Sometimes we can get caught up in the overused word "family". How many times a day do you hear that word referring to a team, a work group or some other gathering? We get the idea and even the feelings involved, but family is a complicated term for us. Does it primarily refer to blood relations?

I don't know what your reaction is when you hear the word tribe, but let's give it some thought. It's hard for us to imagine that idea being relevant in our sophisticated, diverse society. But of course, we have familiarity with the concept through media, as it exists in other cultures.

Tribe evokes images of an ancient social world, perhaps with a tendency to think about it with some condescension. Tribe feels synonymous with primitive. But, there is a lesson to be learned when observing how a tribe functions socially.

Now don't go playing the lunatic card right away; I'm not talking about associations we have with chiefs in tricked out apparel organizing war parties. I'm referring to the tribal model of cohesive, extended family. In its ideal, there is care and protection by each for the others. It's an alternative concept that might be less confusing than family.

We need a tribe, a clan, a gathering. In such terms, it is certainly the right image for us. Perhaps, if finding or creating a new family feels daunting, maybe you need to think about joining a tribe. This is essentially what I've done my entire adult life. I've joined tribes or, if this feels better, communities of convenience. And surely so have you.

The book of Ruth in the Hebrew Bible recounts a poignant story of Naomi, who upon the death of her husband and two sons, decided to return from ten years of exile. One of her daughters-in-law, Ruth, supported Naomi's return but insisted on going with her. Naomi tried to dissuade her by urging her to stay with her "own people." But, Ruth was insistent and her response is well remembered and a quote for the day:

Ruth replied, "Don't urge me to leave you or to turn back from you. Where you go I will go and where you stay I will stay. Your people will be my people and your God my God. Where you die I will die and there I will be buried. May the Lord deal with me, be it ever so severely, if even death separates you and me."[27]

When Naomi realized that Ruth was determined to go with her, she stopped urging her to stay behind. Clearly young Ruthie had psychologically oriented herself to Momma Naomi, as if she were her own mother. She reframed her sense of tribe and family to become Naomi's child when she married her kid. It's a decision; it's not about blood and genes. And this is the heart of it – are you really seeing what tribe of choice is around you?

There are likely social connections available that you might be taking for granted. It starts with reframing or reimagining your connection to groups where you are already a member.

---

[27] The Book of Ruth, third division, *Hebrew Bible: In Ruth 1:16-17*.

These started out as groups and communities of convenience. As Sally states bluntly, "friends are family!"

After high school graduation, I set off to Providence College. From day one in the dorm and on campus I made a seamless transition into a new clan. My freshman cronies soon became my tribe and family. At the time, the college was not co-ed so it was like going off to a monastery, but without the supervision and rules.

For the first time in my life, I was free of parental oversight and it felt like I had ascended into heaven. Here we were, several dozen 18-year-olds adjusting to the transition from family, school and friend relationships and starting all over at the same time. It was great!

These are lifelong friends with whom I am still in contact. You know the cliché about seeing an old friend after many years and being able to pick right up where you left off with laughter and memories? And that is the essence of family, shared experiences you can vividly recall, deeply mourn and where you dissolve in laughter.

When we think about getting socially connected, we have a natural tendency to reach out to those with whom we have compatibility. You relocated to another place and naturally reach out to others that share your interests and profile. You gravitate to your own age group, socioeconomic status and start the family build with the sibling model. It makes sense; it's the path of least resistance.

Now consider for a moment how you linked up with those diverse characters with whom you grew up . Does the idea of finding friendships with people who are the age of your father, grandmother, the uncles and aunts, teenage cousins and children appeal to you? Rarely. If you do eventually wind up in such an extended world, it usually has happened unintentionally, over time and by serendipity. It was not likely a conscious effort, but it most certainly should become your mission.

It's the work of shifting and rebalancing your central life interest, not necessarily interpersonal compatibility. Aren't you related to people to whom you would say, "If I wasn't related to you, I'd probably have nothing to do with you"?

The first comedy club I called home was on Long Island, oddly named 'Richard Dixon's White House Inn'. This club is a legend among comics of that era. It was the starting place for the likes of Eddie Murphy, Rob Bartlett from the Imus Show, Jackie Martling from Howard Stern and local resident Jerry Seinfeld. It was owned by Jim LaRoe, who happened to be a dead ringer for Richard Nixon. The resemblance was amazing. So, he started going around the country with an imposter act. With Watergate came the end of that gig and he used the name Richard M. Dixon when he opened his comedy club in Massapequa.

At the time, I was there seven nights a week, while teaching English at a Catholic High School during the day. From the very beginning, it was obvious that the bond between comics is instant and long lasting. And you can imagine the wild collection of personalities, backgrounds and off-the-wall eccentricities of aspiring comedians. But this was and still is my tribe.

Before long, I moved into New York and began appearing at the Comic Strip Comedy Club on the Upper East Side. After about a year of showcasing, I had enough material to get booked as a full-time professional comic. It was an amazing time in the business, with dozens of us working the circuit. I met and worked with everyone and loved the life of a comedian.

Every night after the show was over, a dozen or so of us hung around the club having drinks and sometimes went to a local diner for breakfast in the middle of the night. We laughed and shared stories and laughed and complained and, did I mention, we laughed? This was my family, formed in the unlikely place of a New York comedy nightclub. Some were destined for fame and others, most perhaps were on the road to good careers somewhere in the bowels of show business as writers, producers, editors and speakers. But to this day, we all share a feeling of belonging to our tribe.

The essence of a tribe is allegiance to the relationships, without abandonment. It means commitment to love, in conjunction with tolerance and forgiveness. Transforming your communities of convenience into a new tribe and family is the natural craving of human beings. And it can take you by surprise.

Our neighbors, Jane and Jeff Boswell, are retired teachers who started offering pottery classes at the local museum. The students have become so engaged and close knit, that every few months they host a get-together called a "pot party". They each bring a dish inside of a dish they made themselves. This community of convenience is now every bit an extended family for them.

It's the transformation from the sadness of finally leaving your home, to the unexpected pleasures found in a retirement home. It's the anxiety of leaving home after high school and being thrown into the most delightful family of college friends imaginable. It's the transition from the fear of that first day of basic training, to the swift bonding with your new band of soldiers.

It's suddenly realizing that your new group of friends caught you by surprise. They came without planning with the person next to you on the treadmill and other machines at the gym, where you went to work on yourself – your individual self. It's the surprising delight you feel when getting to church is no longer about a sense of obligation but an eagerness to see your church family. Tribes are everywhere; families are all around you.

It's about finding people to love in the flesh, not just in the abstract. Human peace and fulfillment follows love.

But wait, there's one more thing.

# CHAPTER 9

# Life Inspired, Life Blessed

Mental health is a phrase now common in our vocabulary. We use it as a character description and sometimes even as an accusation. "She has mental health issues" or "I'm not sure about his mental health." Someone's mental health refers to their current state of functioning and more generally, to their psychological, emotional stability.

The self-discipline required to maintain that stability can be a full-time job. We live in our moods, moment-to-moment, day by day. Managing and adjusting our entangled state of mind is the principle mission for human beings. So naturally, navigating the disruptive rhythms of temperament becomes the focus of psychological intervention. Tweaking our functioning is job one, whether we seek professional help or self-help.

We now see, however, that mental health is really about whole health, the well-being of our body, mind and social context.

As we've outlined, the accepted approach by health professionals when assessing someone's mental health is that ten-dollar term, "biopsychosocial." To fully understand someone's mental health state, we look at them from head to toe and from the skin in. And we take the temperature of their relationship universe. Fine and dandy.

There is a piece missing from the mental health puzzle, however, that can escape us. An assessment of someone's state of well-being should also include consideration of the albeit elusive variable – a spiritual life.

While loaded with religious inference, the word spiritual is not invariably synonymous with any one religious system or dogma. And yet, undeniably, the doctrine of every structured belief system is saturated with the concept of spirituality.

Our use here is about a universal sense of spirit, that permeates all human life. It refers to the meaning we give to our life.

Perhaps our spiritual sense can be seen as the summary interpretation of our biopsychosocial state. Those variables center on the organic and the interpersonal nature of our life in the moment. We now add consideration of our personal reflections. "Here is how I feel about it all."

Let's expand our approach to a "biopsychosocial spiritual" assessment of someone's health. Now, we have a fifty-dollar term. Way better!

So, let's consider our spirit and our spiritual life. Be advised that in our expanded diagnostic system, terms such as spirit and spirituality are variables that elude clear definition and measurement. It is opaque, misunderstood and often repressed; evokes suspicion and is often misused. But its expression is real and critical.

In professional counseling circles, there is always some resistance to drifting into this murky area. A big reason is that it simply resists being clearly defined. My personal sense of spirituality is as distinctive as my DNA. Its variation is evident in how we each describe its meaning and application in our lives.

Consequently, counseling professionals generally have their own unique take on the significance, even the very reality, of this impenetrable matter of spirituality.

Most people don't know the difference between a psychiatrist, psychologist, social worker, psychoanalyst, family therapist ... enough already! Unless you're compelled to understand the distinctions for personal reasons, for most it's, "Who cares?" But in a nutshell (nutshell, see what I did there?), the disciplines each jealously guard their dogmas and turf and the assumptions they were taught in graduate school.

Again, so what? But on this point, you should know that there is a divide among all shrink hotshots about the validity and utility of spirituality and its cumbersome love affair with structured, religious thought.

Some disciplines push back against religious ideology and see it as fishy, purely a "defense mechanism" that should be treated. On the other end of the spectrum are those that embrace the expression of their theological point of view in treatment. And most are banging around somewhere in between. I'm one of those somewhere in the middle, but do lean heavily on my theological viewpoint, shaped through my life experiences.

Why is there this angst about someone's religious ideology clouding the treatment picture? In the psychoanalytic view, belief in God is suspected of being a projection onto an "invented god." Freud even identified this deity as the image of a remote, all powerful father.

Yes, it's weird I know. Nonetheless, if you talk about God with your new analyst and they roll their eyes or snort, be advised that the topic of your religious beliefs may not go smoothly for you there.

Other than those radical types, the state of the field's thinking is that if someone's faith life and religious practice is strengthening emotional well-being and social support, then it's an acknowledged asset, no matter what the therapist personally believes. It's an unfair generalization to dismiss out of hand, the value and strength provided to people in countless, healthy faith communities. In fairness, however, be ready for pushback if your religious liturgy involves chickens, guns, marijuana or human sacrifice.

A factor driving cynicism about some flavors of religion is how it is sometimes publicly shared. This is particularly true with my tradition, the American Christian Church.

When hearing a narrowly educated, incendiary preacher spew outrageous and hateful opinions, humiliating themselves and damaging their mission, the image takes a big hit. Cruel, bullying rhetoric is a poor strategy for welcoming new adherents. But this is what some "preachers" are guilty of doing, often through the media. And anyone can see the gap between their rants and what they know about the Jesus of the Bible.

Being a preacher is a curious profession to say the least. There are many who I admire. And others, I've met who … well, who are other than admirable. At its best, religious practice has profound advantages for elevating and sustaining our spirits. And, keep in mind that religion in American life and culture has added more than just spiritual experiences for individuals.

It has been a robust resource that held communities together and promoted the very social connection that has been lost in America today. People of "the cloth" are supposed to be role models of service, love and humility. It's a high bar. Until we develop robot clergy, expecting this consistency and perfection for a human being, is an unreachably high standard that exposes them to unfair judgement and risk.

Describing someone as a "humble preacher" always seemed an oxymoron. I've always resisted that title – preacher. Although, since I was ordained by a bona fide organization (not just a certificate on the Internet) I could be labeled one. Gag! I earned that status through Union Theological Seminary in New York City, while simultaneously performing each night as a professional comedian and studying at Columbia to be a therapist.

It seemed to me that being a preacher in front of a devoted congregation was similar to being a successful comic. You are in front of a quiet, attentive audience super focused on your every word. But it's without the presence of rude hecklers. It's like show business without all the overt hostility. I demur from the clergy designation and prefer the roles of therapist, teacher, speaker and, yes, comedian. This is my comfort zone.

As much as I have been in a knot about organized religion, there has always been a conviction that the ethical foundation of the Jesus movement is psychologically solid. My own spiritual outlook has been shaped by a combination of Judeo-Christian theology, psychoanalytic and health psychology, counseling and other life experiences.

My sense is that a lot of structured religious systems do a less than adequate job of connecting their orthodox beliefs to the life experiences of people moving about in modern culture. Evidence of this is the stark reality that close to eighty percent of Americans do not participate in church at all. And, while I grew up socialized to understand the esoteric references of my religion, I can imagine what it's like for the uninitiated to "try church" and comprehend the unfathomable language, references and rhetoric embedded in a typical worship experience.

It seems most would be far more likely to attach to systems of insight that resonate within their daily lives. Being physically healthy and emotionally stable are esteemed values that connect more intimately with health and psychological science, than with religion at first blush. Witness the surge in the research and general interest in practices of mindfulness, like meditation and yoga.

It has been in this spirit that I share some observations from my life and career, finding my own path to transcendence. I've done my searching right here in America, making no pilgrimages to a mountain, lighting incense or wearing a robe. I've searched for joy through a lot of formal education and study, interactions with people more brilliant, as well as the daft and the oblivious. And I feel settled in my own mind that I at least know the formula for a happy, balanced life, despite my own spotty record of application.

There are some conclusions I have reached. I was really taken with the work of psychologist Ernest Becker. Raised in Massachusetts by a devout Jewish immigrant family, he served in the Army during World War II. It so happened that his unit liberated a Nazi death camp. One can only imagine the impact of this trauma on Ernest and his fellow soldiers.

After the war, he became a social psychologist and noted scholar. He won a Pulitzer Prize for his 1974 book, *Denial of*

*Death.*[28] He asserted that the fundamental issue of humanity is addressing our mortality. He emphasized our inability to cope with the idea and our response through repression, which in turn exacerbates our individual and, importantly, our collective emotional well-being.

His thesis is compelling, referring to four strands, or braids of existence; the first strand being acknowledgment that nature is full of death. And so it is, alongside the stunning beauty of creation, goes the relentless brutality of remorseless death.

The second braid moves to our acknowledgement that we, as part of nature, will also die. This leads to the third, which asserts that we cannot absorb or accept this cruel reality and so we repress it. And finally, as explained in the fourth braid, human beings characteristically cope with this denial through a projection that emerges in the "character armor" of self-esteem and empowerment. We work toward personal empowerment. And, he goes on to suggest that this pattern essentially, ironically and tragically causes more death!

It is so provocative and yet has the ring of discomforting truth. Our impulse for control and even power, confronts the stated value of humility and service that is embedded in all religious and spiritual systems.

When I read Becker's *Denial of Death* in graduate school, it had a significant impact on my worldview. It resonated with the

---

[28]   Becker, Ernest (1965) *Denial of Death.*

truth for me. But at the same time, it amazingly, enabled me to find a living approach connecting this merciless reality, to what was captivating in the Christian theology of my childhood.

It seemed logical to me, that denial of inevitable death was the core conflict of human life. Nature's barbaric violence reminds us of it. Alongside this insight, I came to understand its relevance to my training as a counselor.

The psychological tenet about the processes of repression and displacement of emotion were seen in the lives all around, including my own. Acts of human ego and grandiosity do often produce outcomes that cause human conflict, cruelty and ultimately deadly consequences.

So, how to respond to this searing insight? Into that system for me came the words attributed to Jesus the Rabbi, who surely not denying the truth of the first three strands, nonetheless beckons us to resist our primal ego reaction. Rather than finding psychic relief by fueling egocentric power, resist this impulse. Opt instead to behave with love and service. This, it seems to me, is the antidote to humanity's murderous proclivities. This is the Way.

It was in this moment, that I put my arms around my Christian faith and it had little to do with the church. It was utterly congruent with the insights and values I learned as a therapist. Being committed to a life of close relationships, to love and service, is the best and right response to the overwhelming anxiety about our fragile existence.

That long-term study on happiness at Harvard referenced earlier, correlated happiness with having a sense of awe about the world and our existence. Where do you look for experiences of awe? The incredible image of your son at his birth? Your newborn granddaughter with some of your face echoed in hers? Is it nature? Where do you look for joy and transcendent meaning?

You can find it in a cathedral or the cathedral of creation in nature found all around us. We fail to see and feel it because of the impulsive nature of our frontal cortex that is in almost perpetual monitoring mode. Noisy minds, raving cognition is what is blocking your view of beauty and awe.

Practicing detachment through meditation and quieting the mind is the way we open ourselves to the awesome existence of the next realities. Again, the Harvard study concluded that the principle variable in a happy life was close social connections. It's being in stable relationships that are not riddled with conflict and harm. And, it expands to include surrounding family, whether related by blood or brought into the close connection like family.

Glenn Sparks and I call them "refrigerator rights relationships." They are the people in your life who have intimacy in your personal space, who can go into your refrigerator without needing permission. Having this social network is the most crucial of all factors for your life and your mood stability. Again chilling cautionary words of the authors: "loneliness kills."

Rebalancing your life and attending to your existence outside work can be done. Because unlike your job, you do have control over this dimension of your life. You can rewire your attitude by growing the quantity and quality of your personal relationships. Extended family is the profile for health and wellness.

As far as tweaking your own mood toward developing a consistent positive attitude, strategies abound. Anxiety is a free-floating discomfort that is often tied up with expectations. And expectations reveal the imbalance between the matter of internal versus external locus of control.

Controlled balance is perhaps best expressed in the serenity prayer of Alcoholics Anonymous: "God grant me the Serenity to accept the things I cannot change, the courage to change the things I can and Wisdom to know the difference."

The science of the past three decades has made vividly clear that practicing mindful exercises has significant impact on our mood and health. Meditation, meditative prayer and yoga, along with exercise don't simply invigorate your muscle tone, they lower your blood pressure, slow your heartbeat and alter your mood. Sally and I practice Transcendental Meditation every day and it has had profound health effects for both of us. It presents no cognitive discord with our faith life.

You have everything you need, even in light of present circumstances, physically and psychologically. What you can change is your social, interpersonal reality. And this is the foundation for spiritual wellness. I urge you to resist that cynicism that accompanies the negative mood and take the counsel of the ages. It's faith, hope and love. If your faith is weak and your hope is lost, in the meantime you can love.

Start there and the others will follow.

It's working for me.

Blessings on your life and your work, now surrender the misery.

# Afterword

Remember the Miserables? What became of them and their miserable situations? Are they still miserable?

## Jack the Miserable Plumber

How did Jack the plumber work out his misery? Recognizing that his job would never guarantee him respect and fulfillment, he turned his life's attention to other activities he loved. He got into cooking, grilling and smoking meats in his "egg" grill. He bought a small boat to take fishing or just idle up on the nearby river.

He also resurrected his love for pottery and helps out at the local art museum for hours at a time. He even climbs up on the roof every November to put up the most tasteful, artsy Christmas lights in the neighborhood.

It has all served to change his attitude, expectations and mood. Then, out of the blue, after five more years, he finally got a promotion. And it was one for which he hadn't even applied! In this new job, his creativity will be vital.

What changed? Hmmm. Maybe he did. He had a new attitude and it showed. Through his creative distractions, he climbed up out of his misery.

## Amanda the Miserable Teacher

How is Amanda doing these days? The daily conversation in the teachers' room was hour after hour of bitter complaining about the pressures on school teachers. The theme was always the same. It was politicians and bureaucrats dictating oppressive testing for young children that interfered with their freedom to teach.

Before long, the repetition and despair was so stressful that Amanda decided to detach herself from the conversation. She chose to put her focus and energy on her classes and students. This is what she could control. Leaving her job behind at the end of the day, she began to feel some mental relief. She turned her thoughts toward her family, neighborhood and church.

She also became active in a yoga class, began meditation, and shifted her focus to health and well-being. She's now in the best emotional shape she's ever been.

## Sean the Miserable Cop

What's up with Sean? He knew he needed some relief from the stress of the job that he carried home after his shift. With the advice of his wife and some friends, he decided to devote more of his free time to an activity that he loved: sports! Specifically, he became involved with every sports activity for kids in his community. He threw himself into coaching baseball, refereeing basketball and even became a coach for his daughter's soccer team.

This new passion enabled him to shift from his very challenging job to the energy and enjoyment of being around active children. In his words, "The moment I changed out of my uniform it was like a switch went off and I was in a happy place. I still love my job, but it's now just my job."

## Nicole the Miserable Nurse Practitioner

Nicole considers herself a nurse 24/7. She just can't get enough of the world of health science and medicine. So, in spite of the frustrations attendant with her job, she is in no way tired of her purpose within the profession.

Although she knew it would add more hours to her week, she decided to take a part-time job at a nearby university as an assistant in their research lab. She got to hang around and commiserate with professors working on a large N.I.H. brain research grant.

She wasn't doing it for the money, which was minimal, but for the exhilaration she felt around these amazing scientists. And she foresees the possibility of this becoming a full-time opportunity when the day comes for her to retire from the hospital. She kept her passion and found her joy.

## Geoffrey the Miserable Company President

There didn't seem to be many options for Geoffrey to change the dynamics at his office. If everyone was essentially an employee reporting to him, who were the peers he could turn to for his support?

His family life was doing nicely, but he needed to change something about the chemistry at his office. He decided on a radical adjustment of attitude and perspective. With the help of a counselor he made a decision to reframe his view of the people who were working around him, even as they were working for him. He realized that his isolation was his undoing.

Slowly he began to reach out to the other executives, even admitting that he would like to develop more of a friendship than simply a business relationship. It started with a weekly lunch with a couple of his vice presidents, expanded to social events with them outside work and before long, they each became more fully engaged with their families.

This simple change propelled him to rethink his psychological approach and altered his emotional experience at work.

## Will the Miserable Comedian

Will had to come to terms with his limitations for mastering the business of show business. After some years of consistent performing, opportunities surely did arise, but these never took him very far. At some point, he came to realize that he simply didn't have the unquenchable passion for show business success that is essential to go to the higher level.

Once he accepted this, it enabled him to widen his perspective and take stock of what he was passionate about for his life. This led him to a variety of professional choices, including public speaking, where he was able to still enjoy his ability as a standup comic.

He went back to graduate school and became a therapist. He got a master's degree in theology and turned his creative energy to writing and podcasting. It took him a long time but he is free from the misery of his job yet still enjoying, even loving his work. If you haven't guessed, yeah, it's me.

In some desperation, each of our miserable workers capitulated and abandoned hope that their job jam was going to turn around. They didn't quit, but emotionally threw in the towel. They couldn't change the other stuff so they chose, in some resignation to take charge themselves.

When they turned their focus to other strategies for coping, they essentially shifted their central life interest from their job and career to their non-work life. And it was here that they found control, possibilities and joy.

Each figured out a way to replace their draining job stress with activities that brought them the gratification that comes with personal empowerment. Their choices, made with surrender, displaced their brooding about work with gratification in new activities.

Since they couldn't fix everything, they decided to fix what they could fix.

And you?

# About the Author

Dr. Will Miller is a psychotherapist and health psychologist, who teaches Strategic Communications at Purdue University. He has worked in Community Mental Health Centers, as well as in drug and alcohol rehabilitation programs. He holds graduate degrees in Urban Education, Theology, Clinical Social Work, and Health Psychology.

For 17 years, Will had an active career as a professional stand-up comedian, headlining clubs across the country. He has made numerous television appearances, including Nick at Nite and host of the NBC Daytime program The Other Side.

Currently, Dr. Miller teaches and speaks to corporations and organizations nationally and is a recognized authority on stress and coping with change. He is the author of several books, including *Refrigerator Rights*, with Dr. Glenn Sparks. His weekly podcast on health and wellness can be accessed at **www.drwill.com**.

Made in the USA
Lexington, KY
24 April 2017